Be Still

How to heal and grow

By

Rev. Winslow Eliot, PhD

BE STILL AND GROW

Cover design and artwork by Jefferson Eliot
http://www.jasperlark.com

Author website by Tom Stier
http://www.tomstier.com

Visit the author website at
http://www.winsloweliot.com

ISBN-13: 978-1-939980-20-5 (paperback)
ISBN: 978-1-939980-21-2 (Kindle)
ISBN: 978-1-939980-22-9 (ePub)
ISBN: 978-1-939980-23-6 (audio)

Published by: Writespa Press

Be Still

Contents

I. Introduction

"There is a presence, a silence, a stillness which is here by itself. There is no doer of it, no creator of this stillness. It is simply here in you, with you."
—Mooji

As a young child living in Greece, I would take my little red chair outside so I could watch the busy ants working in and around their extraordinary anthill. The long line of ants would eventually become completely still in my vision, even though each individual ant was moving. *How strange*, I thought.

When I was a teenager living on the edge of Ashdown Forest, where A. A. Milne wrote his poems and books, I would spend as much time as possible in the woods, "doing nothing," as Christopher Robin so perfectly called it. Through reading and rereading *Winnie-the-Pooh*, I learned about the dichotomy of inner and outer worlds, and that they are one and the same: "Sitting there they could see the whole world spread out until it reached the sky, and whatever there was all the world over was with them in Galleons Lap."

Many decades later, I found myself at a crossroads, even though outwardly there were not many signs of this. All my life I'd been a writer, mainly of novels, and now I was working hard on the third book in a mystery series. I was finding it increasingly difficult to tap into the flow of creativity that I'd come to rely on. My teaching profession, which brought in necessary income, was becoming more stressful and less fulfilling. My mother had recently died. My father was in his mid-nineties and would die soon. My grown children were both far away. My marriage was okay, but my restless dissatisfaction with my life was taking its toll on it.

I'd been interested in metaphysical subjects like tarot, astrology, and palmistry since I was a teenager. They were lifelong hobbies, and it had never occurred to me that my love for metaphysics could be anything more than a hobby.

One day, as I was browsing some hand-reading sites online, I stumbled upon a palmist, Peggy Arvidson, who was offering a three-hour online workshop for "finding your soul's purpose." On a whim, I signed up. The course was rich with information and the group small and lively. But increasingly I felt that the other participants' roadblocks and challenges seemed to me freeing and interesting—even exciting—compared to the fog I was coated by.

At one point, Peggy asked me (as she studied photographs of my handprints that I'd sent her), what my passion *really* was. I felt as though I were falling into a vast hole of nothingness, as I surprised myself by saying, "I want to do nothing. I want stillness. I want to wake up in the morning with absolutely nothing to do, nowhere to go, no one to talk to, and be completely still. I feel as though if I could be still, I'd *know*."

I was half-laughing, embarrassed, a bit hopeless, because although it felt true, it also felt dumb. Who has a passion for doing nothing?

But that was the moment that everything changed. It was as though Peggy—a total stranger— jumped down that dark rabbit hole with me. I felt as though she were holding me as I went down. "That's

a *great* passion!" she said, "and you're not alone —
there's a whole movement out there — there are a lot
of people who feel like you do. Mystics, therapists,
creatives. You need to be a leader in showing other
people how to experience their own stillness. *Follow
your passion.*"

I felt myself landing then, as though on one of the
softest, darkest, quietest pillows of my psyche. With
Peggy's gentle push, I knew what I had to do.

For a long time I'd wanted to go on a stillness
retreat. Now, I dove right in.

Retreat

For three months I retreated into my studio. I
slowed everything down. Way, *way* down.

I didn't write, teach, or socialize. I sometimes
went on quiet, long walks in the countryside where I
live, but otherwise did not venture far from home. I
wanted to explore the value of being still, of allowing
stillness to occur rather than chasing after it.

My stillness retreat became one of the most
significant periods of my life.

I discovered that disconnecting from the incessant

communications and relentless social obligations was the most challenging part of my retreat. I had to work hard to let go of other peoples' expectations that we are—all of us—always available. In our busy, super-connected daily lives, it's easy to inadvertently hurt someone's feelings if we don't respond immediately to requests and invites.

Way back, before the era of cellphones and the internet, when our old landline phone used to ring at dinnertime, we wouldn't answer it. Being together as a family was the priority for that brief hour of the day.

In the same way, during my retreat, I prioritized communications and engagements. I'm still surprised at how hard it was to explain to friends that I had committed to doing nothing and therefore couldn't meet them. Some were amused but most were hurt. Sometimes I had to tell them I was "too busy" because that was the language they understood.

Of course, I knew of people who'd retreated to monasteries or an ashram, or taken a silent pilgrimage to a sacred destination, but these seemed rare, few, and not sustainable ways of experiencing what I wanted to feel in my life on a daily basis. Stillness—not as an escape from my reality but *as* my reality.

My concern that I might be missing something important that was happening in the world at large was also something I wrestled with. For those three months I did not read the news or connect with anyone through social media. It took several weeks for me to realize that the cycles of the seasons continue just the same, even without my being bombarded by urgent news reports and flash updates.

At first, loneliness was also something I had to grapple with. I regretted not choosing to be with other people on a stillness retreat, so we could—even if we were silent—know that we were on a path together. I wanted to be with a tribe who understood my endeavor. I sometimes felt that I was the only person in the world who cared about being still.

After a while, however, the loneliness abated, and eventually transformed into a quiet sense of anticipation. I began to feel as though I were a canvas before it's painted. Or a plot of earth before it's planted. Or a guitar that's being made—not yet being played.

Yet for the entire time there was no sense of waiting. When we're waiting, we aren't fully present. We are waiting for the next thing—a dentist appointment or a date with someone. But during my retreat I wasn't waiting for anything.

I was simply being.

My path through all the challenges and difficulties I encountered during those three months—both inner and outer—was made clear to me through a simple daily ritual:

Every morning I chose a crystal to meditate with, then placed a feather I had found beside it, filled a small glass with water, and lit a candle.

Each evening I put these four items gratefully away.

These items represented, for me, the four elements: A crystal for earth, a feather for air, a vessel for water, and fire as the candleflame. I came to feel that the four elements were all I needed to heal and grow within my space.

They also became the portal through which I connected with stillness. Through supreme rest and security (earth), quieting the mind (air), reaching into the depth of feeling and intuitive wisdom (water), and transmutation and inspiration (fire), I learned to understand stillness.

As the weeks turned into months, a feeling of peace seemed to increase in my little healing studio where I spent most of my time. My old collection of crystals took on a glow I'd never seen before. My many beloved tarot decks revealed stories and insights that shimmered and shifted before my gaze when I spread them out in front of me. Even music I'd listened to a thousand times held a new resonance.

My old beloved books seemed to take on a life of their own. Some I've had since my teens when my interest in metaphysics first emerged. I still have my first palmistry book, by Fred Gettings, and an astrology reference from 1907 I used to consult—it belonged to my great-grandmother. I have a lot of books on Sufism, many books of poetry, and books by Rudolf Steiner, most of which I inherited from my mother, along with her underlines, Post-its, and margin notations. I have tomes on religion and mysticism: Sufism and Islam, Judaism and the Kabbalah, Christian mysticism, Hinduism, and Buddhism. There are plenty of novels and biographies as well, including the novels I wrote myself.

During my retreat, sitting in quiet, reflecting on a question, I'd gaze at a shelf and a title would take on a particular glow, a title that, it turned out, had an answer for me. Another seemed to have a smiling glimmer on its spine and when I reached for it there would be words of guidance for the day or for a friend or for an issue at hand.

And it wasn't just the books: Everything in my studio became animated during those months, as though each item had a life of its own. Everything seemed to have its own consciousness. Throughout the course of my life, I have acquired many beautiful objects—paintings, shells, statues of angels, feathers, gifts I've been given. Many things I've had since I was a child, others belonged to my grandparents or parents. A puzzle box from Florence. A miniature statue of a whirling dervish that I've always loved. An Egyptian stone owl from my father. An old mosaic Turkish coffee set that belonged to my great-grandmother.

All these things became my companions during my stillness retreat. They spoke to me when I needed to hear something. They asked questions I wouldn't have thought up on my own. When I held them in my hands, I felt love emanating *from* them. They became alive.

Research

By the time the three months were over, I had fallen in love with the long, quiet hours of night and day, a powerful rhythm of meditation, accomplishing daily chores mindfully, long walks in nature, and pleasurable resting in between. I did not want my retreat to end.

But the holidays were approaching, and I was also getting increasingly interested in the metaphysics of stillness. Was it possible that stillness could be as healing and empowering for others as well as myself? I imagined it could be, but didn't know why or how. What were some of the ways each one of us could learn to use stillness for healing, personal development, counseling, spiritual growth, and the ins and outs of daily life?

What I learned, as I delved into the possibilities and potentialities that stillness offered, was that I was not alone in my love for stillness. Many other people regarded it as a path to inner peace and spiritual development. I rediscovered mystics like stillness guru Eckhart Tolle and the writer Pico Iyer, yoga teachers like Erich Schiffman, craniosacral practitioners like Charles Ridley, and I read Lao-Tsu and other Taoists (including *The Tao of Pooh*) with a new understanding.

The way stillness works, I learned, was through allowing healing to take place—allowing it physically, mentally, emotionally, and spiritually.

The 'allowance' is not passive but receptive, a difference I had not understood before my retreat.

It continues to astound me how much research has been done already on the efficacy of stillness as a healing modality and a spiritual path. In a world that seems to measure itself by other peoples' standards, to revolve around busyness and accomplishment, with an emphasis on competition and success, and an insistent need for constant interaction and engagement, I thought I was the only one who believed that quietness and stillness were key to health and well-being, much less a transcendent experience of connection with our spirit.

Additionally, all the metaphysical tools I'd used since adolescence became my allies and friends. Astrology became a loving relationship with the stars as, sitting outside on my deck, I admired the night sky. And as I turned over a tarot card to meditate on it, I felt as though I were entering a miniature universe.

The one aspect that did not end at the close of the three months was my morning and evening ritual of connecting with the four elements. They became a powerful catalyst in structuring my work with stillness, so that it crystallized out of the swirl of metaphysical techniques that up until now I thought

I knew well.

They became so much a part of my work and structure that I began exploring the relationship between earth, air, water, fire, and stillness. I came to understand that it was through the four elements that any experience of stillness could be accessed and activated in our daily lives.

What is the core experience of being consciously still? *Becoming aware of being aware.* When we become aware of our awareness in each of our four bodies — physical, mental, emotional, spiritual — we are assured of healing and well-being.

Practice

Thinking back, I don't know how it happened, but before long, people began to come to see me, asking for guidance. First a friend wanted advice about something, and then her friend came by with a question. Within a few weeks, more and more people were calling me to schedule a tarot session or asking me to read their hands. They would enter my little oasis, as I called it, and look around almost in wonder before they began to speak their troubles. I would tuck them onto my couch with a soft blanket, show them how they could become relaxed and still physically (earth), then calm their anxious mental chatter (air) with a guided meditation. Once their feelings (water) grew more quiet and still, we were able to transform (fire) their issue or challenge into clarity or direction.

I remind my visitors that they are travelers, and that they are welcome to rest and refresh themselves in my oasis. Here, they can feel safe and nourished, and they can allow themselves to relax. It's not a place for them to stay—it's a place for replenishment, encouragement, direction, and empowerment. They can rest, and benefit from the healing power of stillness. They can feel the love I feel for them and thus feel it for themselves.

My career as a metaphysical practitioner flourished so quickly I'm still surprised and awed. In addition to my own stream of clients, I was soon offered a part-time position at a high-end wellness resort where I lecture regularly on metaphysics and offer workshops and classes.

Then a couple wanted me to officiate their marriage and, as one thing tumbled after another, I became ordained as an interfaith minister. After that, I got my master's degree in metaphysics and began researching and writing my PhD dissertation—on stillness, for a degree in transpersonal counseling.

I continue my studies and my practice as a metaphysical practitioner, mostly centered around palmistry, astrology, and tarot, as well as a delve into world religions, sacred geometry, crystals, and sound and color therapies. I've gotten certifications in hypnotherapy, angel readings, mediumship, and Waldorf education, which is based on the mystic Rudolf Steiner's anthroposophical worldview. The more I learned and the more I practiced, the more I realized that the actual portal we use for metaphysical healing work does not matter nearly as much *as the way we use that portal*. And the best way to use it is with the absolute, clear understanding that love is at the heart of all we do and are.

Answering that singular desire, voicing my passion on that phone call to a woman I'd never met, a passion that initially made me feel embarrassed, changed everything. I knew who I was and what I wanted to be doing—by allowing stillness to rise clearly within me.

II. The Potential of Stillness

Where Do We Come From? What Are We? Where Are We Going? –Paul Gauguin

When I began to practice full time as a metaphysician, I experienced firsthand how stillness aids the therapeutic process and how its effects last far beyond the time a client and I are together.

It is in stillness, for example, that the opacity of the images and symbols on tarot cards dissolves into a super-focused lucidity. Tarot is a system of symbols, images, and archetypes in a card deck that works on our unconscious much in the way dreams do, by clarifying or giving insight into a situation, relationship, or decision. When they're read from a place of stillness, it's as though scratched, grungy windowpanes are power-washed and I can see *through* the cards with utter clarity.[1]

During my sessions, I sometimes hear myself saying, "There it is—the Stillness—do you feel it too?" And the client nods and grows quiet and understands that they need to let the image on the tarot card to do its therapeutic work, with my hardly needing to interpret or guide.

This experience occurs too when I hold their hands during a palmistry session or as I gaze at their birth chart and the stars come to animated life in the grace of stillness.[2]

I believe that this clarity occurs in large part because it through being still that we can bring to consciousness that which is unconscious.

Working with Stillness

Although my expertise is mainly in tarot, astrology, palmistry, and other metaphysical practices, stillness imbues all my therapeutic sessions. I have discovered that during stillness we can explore our earliest memories, we can connect with our higher selves, and we can glimpse our future potentials. We can experience healing from past wounds, forgiveness and release, and freedom from suffering, And we can connect with our soul's purpose.

I've found that answers to the essential questions we all, at one time or another, ask ourselves—"Who am I? Why am I here?"—are revealed in the silence of stillness. Each one of us can experience stillness on our own, at any time, in every place.

Through my research into ways of accessing stillness in myself and in others, I developed a process and structure for engaging with stillness that anyone can use to heal and grow. It is based on the premise that we can access stillness through the wisdom of the four elements, which correlate with our physical, mental, emotional, and spiritual bodies.

Through becoming physically still (earth), mentally still, calm, objective, and clear (air), emotionally still in an intuitive flow of loving what is (water), and allowing creativity and mystical passion to move us (fire), these four bodies become integrated, so that we can discover who we are and what our life purpose is.

Finding stillness and being able to live in stillness, no matter how fiercely life rages around me, has become my passion. And helping others to experience this has become my mission.

Earth, Air, Water, and Fire

Awareness is a mirror reflecting the four elements. —Thich Nhat Hanh

We are made of earth, air, water, and fire. These four elements are the essence of our humanness from birth to the moment of our final exhalation. Our physical body (earth), our emotional body (water), our mental body (air), and our creative spirit (fire) need to be in balance in order for us to feel healthy.

Thus, experiencing stillness in these four bodies, or elements, can be used to build a solid foundation for healing and personal development in anyone and everyone.

Imagine your life as a building with four sides. In the tarot, four is the number of stability, security. It's the number that signifies our Earth. Four corners. Four seasons. Four directions on our compass.

When we allow stillness to permeate the four elements within us, we can self-repair. We become whole. We can grow. We can thrive.

We all encounter times when we need renovation, restoration, or a new perspective. Stillness allows that. Stillness is like the scaffolding that supports you through your life. It allows you to redesign and reconstruct. It allows you to show up in your fullest expression of yourself.

Being in stillness can heal us in these specific ways:

Physically (earth body), it calms the heart rate and lowers the blood pressure.[3]

Mentally (air body), it helps to quiet the busy—and sometimes harsh—mental chatter that can often be debilitating psychologically.[4]

It can also be a way to become emotionally connected to the flow of our intuition, so that we can access our wisdom, as Lao-Tsu and the Taoists show (water body).

Ultimately, spiritual stillness can flood us with mystical peace, connecting us to universal consciousness or Source (fire body).

Thus, I have connected the therapeutic uses and practical applications of stillness into four:

- **Earth:** stillness in the *physical body* and developing our relationship with nature.
- **Air:** stillness in the *mental body*; mindfulness, and how paradoxical thinking can dissolve the cloudiness of mind pollution (over-thinking, over-analyzing, worry, etc.).
- **Water:** stillness in the *emotional body*; the flow of intuitive wisdom and how love permeates everything.
- **Fire:** stillness in the *creative body*; transformation through what I regard to be the five main initiations of human experience (birth, adolescence, falling in love, sickness, and death) and the mystical experience of knowing ourselves through igniting stillness within.

Element	Body	Stillness	Outcome
Earth	Physical	Embryogenesis, Nature	Health, wellbeing
Air	Mental	Mindfulness, paradoxical thinking	Clarity, insight
Water	Emotional	Intuitive wisdom, love	Flow, peace
Fire	Creative	Initiations of birth, adolescence, falling in love, sickness, and death	Transformation, growth

Integrating these four bodies through stillness can help each one of us to evolve into increased health and well-being. In stillness, we lift the veil to reveal our inner intelligence, the wisdom that knows what we need in order to be healthy, balanced, directed, and fully committed to our soul's purpose, our highest potential.

Time and Space

"In the stillness of your presence, you can feel your
own formless and timeless reality as the
unmanifested life that animates your physical
form." — Eckhart Tolle

Before we dive into the four elements and see how they can lead us into this magical, healing world of stillness, let's explore what stillness is.

Imagine yourself as an undeveloped photograph in an old-fashioned darkroom. As the photograph is developed, the image appears. But the image itself was created already, by the photographer and their trusty camera. In the same way, your essential nature is not a process or a development. You already *are* that image that develops, when you allow it to.

Much of our so-called suffering occurs when we try to develop into something we are not or try to change our image to fit a preconceived idea or expectation. But the innate image of our humanness already exists. It exists in a timeless, space-less reality. Being alive consists of allowing that image to become more and more visible, three-dimensional, and beyond.

Stillness is like the darkroom, and can help in

developing the essential image that is *you*.

Part of our understanding of stillness occurs when we shift our consciousness away from a concept of linear time. Instead, imagine that stillness itself is its own realm, outside the realm of time. Even more importantly, there is always plenty of time, because we can create all the time we need.[5,6]

James Hillman describes it this way: "For this is the nature of an image, any image: It's all there at once. When you look at a face before you, at a scene out your window, or a painting on the wall, you see a whole gestalt. All the parts present themselves simultaneously."[7]

Understanding the whole gestalt can happen in an instant, or an hour, or a lifetime, but it exists in stillness. It just is. And when we recognize it, we also recognize our potentiality.

That whole gestalt resides in stillness, in which our wisdom can be accessed and activated. Even traumatic events or physical injuries contain a seed of stillness that, when allowed to exist by being nurtured and trusted, can enable healing to occur. We are naturally beings of motion and action, but stillness is equally present.

I am reminded of this when I meet someone who is super-ambitious. Their future defines them—their hearts are always yearning and planning. For example, Morgan was a client who, until recently, had been a successful financial advisor. She had her entire future planned, she thought, which included marriage, children, and a swift return to her career. Due to fertility issues, she had made sure to have several embryos frozen. When she came to see me, she already had brought one of those embryos to term and had a healthy child who was five years old. But what should she do with the embryos that remained? She wanted to return to work, as she and her husband had planned.

"What are your options?" I asked her.

"I suppose we could donate them for research," she sighed.

"Or?"

"I could try to bring any that the doctor thinks are viable to term and have more children." She shuddered, and then went on to tell me that her pregnancy was the worst experience in her life. "I was terribly sick. Had to lie down the entire time—in a lot of pain from hernias and gastric issues. It took me months to recover. Also, I had to stop working and I love my work."

I wondered whether there was any ideology at the basis of her dilemma or whether her question had more to do with her own health. "Could you tell me about your religion or spirituality?" I asked.

"We're not religious but I'd say we're both spiritual. We do yoga and things."

"Your relationship with your husband is good?"

"Yes. He says he'll support any decision I make."

I asked about the option of a surrogate parent.

She shook her head firmly. "No, we wouldn't trust someone else to make the necessary health choices."

"What about offering the embryos to someone else who can't have their own baby?"

She shook her head again. "We wouldn't be comfortable knowing a child of ours was alive but we weren't in contact … It would be like giving them up for adoption."

My work as a metaphysical practitioner is not to try to persuade someone to do anything they don't want to do. It's also not my place to argue with anyone's convictions, no matter how opposed they might be to my own. My job is to help the person sitting in front of me to become clear about what their own heart is telling them, what their life's path is, without regard to outside influences of a supposed right or wrong answer, family or marital pressures, or financial insecurity.

My job was to try to help this woman in front of me to sort out her mixed feelings about a complex situation. I had a strong sense that something was shifting dramatically inside her as we talked. She was going to have to move forward in a way that was different to how she'd imagined.

"If you decide not to bring them to term," I said, "you could have a funeral for each of them. Do you think you would grieve?"

There was a long silence as she contemplated the question.

"Yes, I think I would grieve," she said at last.

"What would you be grieving?"

"I look at my kid now and see him so alive and so full of love, and the love we feel for him." She sighed. "But I just don't know if I can go through another pregnancy, much less several."

I was silent. Stillness began to imbue the conversation.

"Some won't be viable, of course," she said. "I probably wouldn't have to have all of them."

I stayed quiet.

"So can you tell me what I should do?" she asked. "What my course of action is? Do you see my future?"

While we were talking, I was seeing her more and more clearly as a loving, conscious being, aware of how her actions would ripple out into the future. I also saw how desperately she wanted to make the right decision for herself, her family, and her as yet unborn children. She'd become distinct to me, like the photograph developing in the darkroom. All I needed was for this lovely, confused woman to see herself as clearly as I did.

"We're going to go on a time travel journey," I told her. "Are you ready?"

Through a guided visualization, I led her into an inward forest, down a great mossy spiral staircase, counting thirty steps into the future from her current age. "Thirty-nine, forty, forty-one, forty-two ..." I counted smoothly, gently guiding her into her own core of stillness.

Eventually, we were standing at the bottom of the stairs in a forest glen. There was sunshine pouring through thick green leaves and friendly birds singing. "Now see yourself in thirty years. You're sixty-eight years old."

I let that sink into the stillness of the meditation for a moment.

"You're going to imagine yourself at sixty-eight in each of the following scenarios. First, see yourself remembering the funeral you gave each of these embryos. See yourself weeping."

I paused to give her time to feel this. Then I continued:

"Now, I want you to put aside your grief—place it under a nearby tree. Good. In this new scenario, remember back to how you let your husband and doctor take care of the business of donating the embryos to science. You've returned to your job, the work that you enjoyed so much. You have clients who value you and you are highly successful in your job."

I paused again.

"Take a moment to absorb what that feels like. Good … When you're ready, place that one under the tree with the other one. You'll come back to them later. Now I want you to imagine yourself at sixty-eight years old again. You're looking back on your life. Remember your pregnancies—not the one you already went through, but perhaps a few more. We don't know how many, but we know you've opted to try to have more children. Remember the suffering you felt, the sickness, the pain. Remember the joy and the love. Remember all of it from your current age of sixty-eight. You have several grown-up children."

She nodded again. We were together in a place of such stillness I could smell the mossy ground and the bark of the trees. I was pretty sure she could too.

"Good. Now put that one down too, along with the others. Now here's a different memory: you gave your embryos to people who couldn't have their own children and longed for a family. They've raised them in their own way and the children have lives of their own that you know nothing about. But they're loved and taken care of, and they're alive."

Her eyes were still closed. We sat together in contemplative silence for several more minutes. Then I guided her back up the mossy stairs so she was back in her current age and place.

She exhaled a sigh—resignation or relief, I couldn't tell which. I told her to open her eyes when she was ready.

Her eyelids fluttered open. "I get it," she said.

"Describe to me what you saw," I suggested. "Do you know now what to do?"

"Yes." There was not an iota of her previous confusion in her eyes. She gazed at me steadily. "We're going to have more children."

I nodded. "What helped you to see that?"

"When I'm sixty-eight, I don't want look back on my life and say, hey, look at how much money I made for this person or that person. And I don't want to wonder if every child I encounter might be my own— I can't give them up to anyone else. I want to be surrounded by children and maybe even grandchildren ... beings of love. It's now so obvious."

Through becoming still, she was able to see the various potential outcomes, or photographs, of each choice she could make. In this way, she could see clearly what she wanted to manifest for her future.

She'd found her answer by being in the stillness of seeing herself as who she developed into thirty years from now. It wasn't a linear journey—it was a journey of becoming.

She'd seen the various photographs of her future developing before her eyes, and recognized the one that felt distinctly hers.

Stillness in Motion

"Everything that is alive has within it a principle of motion and of stationariness." — Aristotle

Life as we know it could not exist without both motion and stillness.[8] Since each living thing has within it the potential of both movement and stillness, and this fact is at the heart of change and growth, we need to consciously experience both.

Most people are familiar with being in a state of motion. Humans tend to 'do' pretty easily. Even when procrastinating, we are *actively* procrastinating. We tend to be overactive mentally, mulling over the past or worrying about the future.

These are all active, or motion, states.

Being in stillness, on the other hand, is rare, and the healing aspect of stillness is necessary in order to grow, transform, and be at peace, too. This is because our nature combines both movement *and* stillness. A person is the material aspect and their continually manifesting growth and development. Combine the two, and we have a human being.

We are each both a noun and a verb *at the same time*.

We need to *become stillness.*

The sea is the sea (noun) and at the same time it is motion of constant waves, currents, and tides (verb). The air is air, but in motion it is the wind; it is both stillness and motion. In stillness, we are both object (noun) and the object in motion (verb), simultaneously. The paradox of being *and* becoming is at the heart of being still.[9]

Moreover, stillness is not just a verb (being still) that connects us with our inner being, or Source, it *is* our inner being *and* Source. Stillness is not just an experience we access during a session; stillness is our *innermost* nature.

It is our wisdom, our consciousness, our intelligence. Through stillness, everyone can experience themselves, or their singular 'I', as the becoming—the verb.

Finding Our True Nature

*"'By nature' the animals and their parts exist, and
the plants and the simple bodies (earth, fire, air,
water)—for we say that these and the like exist 'by
nature'." Aristotle*

We are all subject to the laws of stillness and change just as each particle of nature blooms into its own signature potential. Everything has a consciousness of becoming itself, according to its own nature.

As we know, the nature of a flame is to go upward; the nature of water is to flow downward and to find its own level. In the same way, every human being has their own individual nature.

Furthermore, everything alive has the potential to become its fullest nature—like the potential we see in an acorn to become a huge oak tree.[10] It's in stillness that we can discover our individual nature, the actuality and substance of who we are—our signature or potentiality.

Let Go, Let Stillness

*"This is love: to fly toward a secret sky, to cause a
hundred veils to fall each moment. First to let go of
life. Finally, to take a step without feet." —Rumi*

The secret to the therapeutic and enlightening gift
of stillness lies in accepting it, surrendering to it,
accepting the stillness that is already within you.

In stillness, an opening occurs that allows your
essential nature to reveal itself, an understanding of
your soul's purpose, and an experience of your
connection to Source. Your healing, well-being, and
spiritual development emerges naturally.

Stillness is far more healing and enriching than
just the quieting of the mind or the gentleness of calm.
When we surrender to stillness within ourselves, we
let our true health and wholeness to manifest.

We also realize that stillness *is* our signature
nature.

Be Still, and Know

*"The Reasonists held the maxim of 'I think,
therefore I am.' But the body's truth is actually, 'Be
still and know I am.'* —Charles Ridley*

'Be still, and know' became my mantra throughout my exploration into stillness as a healing modality. I found myself surrendering to the research, the thoughts, the ideas of mystics, scientists, and transpersonal psychologists in ways that took me farther into stillness than I ever imagined I could go.

Be still and know also became the outcome of my exploration. I discovered that stillness is at the core of every aspect of our lives and permeates every aspect of our being. What I've always regarded as the five most significant "initiations" of our earthly existence (birth, adolescence, love, sickness, and death) became infused with the transformative experience of stillness. I saw how stillness not only makes us more peaceful but more alive.

Through stillness we not only heal ourselves, but we connect to our essence.

We not only connect to our essence, but we recognize our highest human potential.

We not only connect with our highest human

potential, but we move (and are motionless at the same time) into its sublime fulfillment.

We are *on* the way and we *are* the way.

I discovered for myself the heart of this mystical paradox: that we are both the Being and the Becoming *at the same time.*

During some light-hearted forays into the mind-blowing research of quantum physicists, I discovered how connected mystics and quantum physicists are: they both have the same point of reference, which is consciousness.[11]

When we become still, we are utterly aware of being aware. Nothing else exists; just the now. And in the now, there is no aging, no disease, no death. Might that be the grace of healing through stillness? That dis-ease and death do not exist even in our so-called physical reality? Metaphysician Stephen Harrison suggests that it may be so:

> "Reality only exists at this meeting point and because of this meeting point. We are both the expression of consciousness and the embodiment of it in the materiality. Consciousness without the material has no expression, the material without Consciousness has no reality. Neither has existence without the other."[12]

Stillness intertwines the healing of mind, body, and spirit. It teaches us how to be aware of being aware. It helps in the development of human consciousness. It reveals to us the profound paradoxes of "all that is without is within and all that is within is without," and "all that moves is still and all that is still is in motion."

What is particularly wonderful is that stillness can be accessed through our foundational human experience of the four elements: earth, air, water, and fire.

III. The Four Elements

*"Give up the notion that 'I am so and so.' All that
is required to realize the Self is to be still. What can
be easier than that?" —Ramana Maharshi*

E ach one of us exists in a four-fold human experience
that is a rich mixture of our physical, psychological,
emotional, and spiritual selves. When we integrate
these in a healthy, balanced, holistic way, we can
heal, we can grow into our fullest potential, and we
can thrive as developing human beings.

These four energetic bodies can be correlated with

the four elements:

- earth/physical
- air/mental
- water/emotional
- fire/spiritual.

In stillness, these four bodies become integrated within us, so that we can discover our own "I am that I am" through the work of "be still and know."

Through the stillness that is present in these four bodies, each of us can find our way toward wholeness, creative expression, and spiritual adventure. I've found that experiencing stillness in one dimension opens the portal to stillness in all dimensions.

Pick the area of stillness you need in your current moment or what you're interested in. You don't have to be still in all areas at the same time—working with stillness is not about arriving at something or accomplishing preset goals!

What I provide are options for you to explore, not rules to live by. Once you've tasted mental stillness, for example, it continues to expand and grow in other areas that you may not yet imagine.

In all our encounters with our fellow humans, we see vividly how different people are, and how each of us may take a different path through (what sometimes feels like) the dark woods of our psyche in our search for well-being, clarity, or peace. Stillness can be a helper, a healer, or a guide.

In the next four sections, I show how stillness manifests in and can transform the four bodies of the human being. In stillness we can perceive clearly our emotional and psychological blocks, tap into a well of intuitive knowing that is not muddied by mental chatter, and penetrate the mystery of our true nature as well as our connection to our spirit and Source.

Earth—Stillness in the Physical Body

"Whenever you begin to have a feeling that
something is not right with the health of the body,
you should become as quiet and still as possible,
both physically and mentally." —Dr. Leon Masters

Our Planet Earth

Our beautiful planet is the place where we ground ourselves, where we feel secure and safe. We experience the earth through our five main physical senses, and relish the wonder of fragrance, taste, shape and color, sound, and touch that it provides.

Our planet represents sustenance and shelter.

She is our mother and our home.

We are all connected to the great web of life on this earth, from the ancient glaciers and highest mountains, to the tiniest insect; from the interrelatedness of our natural world to the six (or fewer) degrees of separation that connect each one of us with another human being.

As Tam Hunt writes in *Scientific American*, the newly-developed resonance theory of consciousness suggests that resonance, or synchronized vibrations, "is at the heart of not only human consciousness but of physical reality more generally."[13]

This means we are all connected and everything that exists on our exquisite planet is—to some degree—conscious.

We are entities who are developing consciousness and self-awareness through our physical experience of being on this planet. The earth teaches us how to appreciate beauty, kindness, work, and each other, as well as survival.

It teaches us about belonging, because we can only become conscious of belonging if we are conscious of feeling "separate from." Dualism may be at the heart of human suffering. We have to experience dualism, because it is the only way we can learn about individuation. This is the transformation that occurs when our unconscious (personal and collective) is assimilated into our personalities and we become integrated, whole human beings. We must feel separated in order to experience connection.

I realized this early on when my travel-hungry parents would move us to a new country: I gained consciousness of my individuality through being abruptly separated from my surroundings. Who was I, without the people and environment I felt were part of me? Homesickness taught me about separation and individuation. Some people first grow conscious of feeling separate and lonely when they fall in love, or desire something that expands their perception of themselves.

But I also found that when we need to heal from the fragmentation of this human experience of being separated and alone, we can always return to our signature wholeness.

As we've established, we can access this experience of wholeness through stillness.[14]

Before We Were Born

> *"The self must know stillness before it can discover its true song."* —*Ralph Brum*

Our remarkable, healing state of active stillness has its genesis, quite literally, in the womb, while the embryo is created, forming, and developing.

Charles Ridley, in his book called *Stillness: Biodynamic Cranial Practice and the Evolution of Consciousness*, describes how the motion of the growing embryo attracts and guides molecules from a chaotic periphery toward the central stillness of the midline.

During the first two weeks following conception, the embryo is amorphous protoplasm. "It possesses no structures, but is a clear-as-glass liquid crystal matrix. Then, around day fourteen, its signature pattern proceeds to organize the cells that produce a visible line in the center of the embryo, called the primitive streak, and the first visible midline appears. *The core of the primitive streak is stillness.*"[15]

If stillness is a basic principle of embryogenesis, wouldn't it thus make it also a principle of adult health and healing? I believe so.

As the embryo grows, it requires both stillness and growth to exist in and around itself so that the rest of the body develops in tandem. For example, the brain grows fast and the heart grows more slowly, and they work in motion and in stillness to evolve together. Craniosacral therapist, Michael J. Shea, describes how

> It is beautiful to ... realize how many areas of stillness
> are in the embryo. The heart itself is another good
> example of this metabolic stillness. ... The heart,
> because of all the bending and folding it undergoes in
> its development, has numerous stillpoints everywhere
> there is a bend or a twist in it. Even the walls of the
> veins and arteries have such restraining functions and
> thus stillness.[16]

Before long, the embryo knows that there's a 'me' and there's a 'you,' in the sense that it creates a self-recognition system that summons an immune response to anything it recognizes is not 'me.' Even before we are born, our little growing fetus has to feel "separate." In order to survive, we need to protect ourselves from anything that is different from us.

This becomes a pattern in every aspect of our being for the rest of our lives: we are born with an innate capacity for self-recognition. A foreign substance, whether it's a germ, or a strange sound, or someone telling us to behave differently than we want to, gets us responding physically or emotionally in defense of *who we are*.[17]

Yes, recognizing self from nonself is a vital function for survival. But it can also result in loneliness, feeling like an outcast, and possibly even despair.

Dualism, the feeling of separation from the 'other,' that we all experience, is the basis for all our longing, desire, disharmony, and dis-ease.

It is the all-too-familiar experience of being human.

Part of the healing magic of stillness comes from accepting the innate coherence of being whole *and* separate. We can accept this paradox through knowing, listening to, and trusting our bodies. When we do, we experience stillness.

During my opening meditation before sessions with clients or before any creative endeavor I undertake on my own, I make sure my body is as comfortable as I can make it. I adjust even the tiniest toe to make sure it is relaxed. I relax my jaw and eyes. It's hard to trust stillness if we don't trust our bodies! Becoming completely relaxed and calm in every cell is a good place to begin.

By creating a quiet space for our physical bodies to be relaxed, we can feel ready and open to stillness. In that moment of relaxation and anticipation, we listen, notice, and allow a gentle receptivity, *an active stillness*, to rise up from within.

Relax into Stillness

"To have faith is to trust yourself to the water.
When you swim you don't grab hold of the water,
because if you do you will sink and drown. Instead
you relax, and float." –Alan Watts

We all experience stillness at various times, but typically they occur as moments of grace, random and fleeting feelings of integration. What I try to do when I meditate into stillness, or during healing sessions, or even moments of crisis, is to allow stillness to imbue the situation.

Each one of us can induce stillness in ourselves and our surroundings. When we relax our physical bodies, we become still. Then we become receptive to stillness.

There is no chasing after it or forcing it. When given the opportunity, it comes naturally. The feeling of stillness is as though a mesh screen has been lifted from the situation and every sense is bathed in a clearer light. The most remarkable aspect of stillness becomes our conscious awareness of it, while at the same time being one with the stillness itself. It is almost as though we have moved beyond being one-with-everything *and* beyond duality into a new realm of consciousness.[18,19,20]

One day a client came to me with this all-too-familiar question:

Should I leave my husband for the man I love?

"First tell me a little about yourself," I began.

Sitting straight and pale, speaking in a low, trembling voice, she told me her husband was a reserved, harsh, much older man who had never loved her. He was seventy, she in her early fifties. She was from a country that had strict laws against adultery, but recently she'd fallen in love with a younger man, the same age as her son. In fact, her son and this man were good friends.

"But does he love me or does he just want my money? I am very rich."

I felt I needed to help her avert the potential disaster that would occur if she pursued her romantic dream. In other words, it did not matter whether or not this young man loved her or was after her money. In this instance, I wasn't being asked to save her marriage, but her life.

"Should I leave my husband? I hate him so much."

She was concretely focused on a yes-or-no response from me, and I tried to help her see the in-between.

"There's no 'should' here," I said. "We need to find out what's best for you."

She looked disappointed. "So you can't see the future?"

"The future is only potential until it's created, and then it's the present. What we need to 'see' are all your potential outcomes and then you get to choose, in freedom, what your future is."

This response did not appear satisfying to her. I could tell she wanted a fortune-teller, not a metaphysical practitioner, but I also felt I could help her see clearly what she needed to decide to do. I drew my crystal ball so that it was placed between us. It's one of my favorite tools for getting centered, grounded, and letting things show up as they are — at least, that is how I usually experience the wonderful healing power of crystal gazing.

I sensed this lovely woman was ungrounded and desperate and I tried to untangle some of the strands of her misery so we could examine them separately.

"Does the young man know your feelings?"

Yes, she replied, and he was as in love with her as she with him, even though he was still only in his late twenties. "I have not been unfaithful yet," she sighed. "I try to resist." The implication was that it was just a matter of time.

"What would happen if you gave in to your attraction?" I asked.

"My son would be very angry if he found out. Perhaps I would never see him again. I don't know if I could bear that. And I would be expelled from my husband's family of course. But I don't care about that." She paused. "My husband—he would probably want to kill me."

She looked so stricken and weak that I brought her a glass of water.

"You're safe here," I said, matter-of-factly, "and here and now is all that exists. Tell me about your home. What does it look like?"

"It's beautiful, of course, and very large. My husband has his quarters and I have mine, so we very rarely see each other. Can you tell me when he is going to die? Perhaps I can wait till then."

"Seeing" when someone might die is not the point of a healing metaphysical session—the point is to learn how to live now. I tried to explain this to her.

"My boyfriend sings to me at night from the courtyard outside my window," she mused, dreamily. "And one day I awoke and he had strewn hundreds of red and pink roses all around my house, right up to the front door. But does he really love me or does he just want my money? I am very, very rich, you know."

I shook my head. "It doesn't matter whether he is in love with you. What matters is *you*. Look at yourself, look at your life. You are beautiful, wealthy, safe."

"But I'm so unhappy," she wept. "My husband is so strict, so mean to me. He does not love me. Does my boyfriend really love me? Can you see that?"

We had been going around in circles, solidly entrenched in her longing to be told that a future with her lover would have a happy ending.

But I couldn't tell her that.

I tried to be gentle. "In ten years, you'll be sixty-six years old. And he will be thirty."

I was stating a fact. The earthy crystal clarity in the ball in front of me was centering me so that I didn't get swept into her stormy waves of suffering. My words weren't logical, nor emotional, nor was I giving her advice. I just wanted her to see things as they were—not as she wished they would be. Before now, she was focused on the urgency of her desire, of her dream of being romanced by this young lover. But even if she survived execution, she still had to consider the passage of time. "He might want children, a family. How would you feel about sharing him?"

She burst into tears again. "I can't let him do that!"

She looked so sad that I realized I had to change tactics. I needed to ground her not just in reality but in potentiality. I needed to show her how the planet we live on is more beautiful and good than it felt to her just then. I needed her to see its richness and possibilities.

"You need to have more fun," I said, after a while, when her sobs began to abate. "To take more pleasure in outside things."

"I have no friends," she replied.

"It's time to get behind a cause, something you care about. Could it be hungry children who you would like to help? Or an artistic company that you could support, a museum perhaps? All your passion and hunger for love needs to be channeled into creative, helpful, loving outlets. What are some opportunities that are available to you that you could throw your heart into?"

"I write poetry sometimes," she murmured, looking a bit ashamed.

"Wonderful! Then can you offer a weekly poetry salon, for instance. Perhaps you could even start up a small little publishing house that publishes beautiful poetry—your own and your friends'. Bring culture and art and people into your life. Something you love doing and sharing."

"I like my poems, it's true. But they are all love poems."

"Love can be beautifully inspiring! Make something real and tangible from your heart's longing. Have more fun."

Her tears were finally dry, and she nodded acquiescently as she put on dark sunglasses. She probably knew from the beginning that her question was not whether or not she should leave her husband for her lover. Of course she knew that was not possible in her world.

Her question was, "How can I live on this earth feeling such despair and loneliness?"

And through the stillness of our physical earth, grounding her in space and bringing her into the present time, I hope she was given a helping hand and perhaps even a stepping-stone toward joy.

Vibrate into Stillness

*"If you want to find the secrets of the universe,
think in terms of energy, frequency, and vibration."*
–Nikola Tesla

Do you experience physical matter as firm, solid, even immovable or unchangeable? Most of us do. We stub our toe on the table leg. We build houses out of wood, brick, cement—solid materials that guarantee security.

But there is another way to understand our physicality, and that is as energy. Energy is constantly pulsating, changing, and vibrating.

Our physical existence on this planet is not so solid and dense as we might think it is. We are shimmering, dancing particles that have grouped together to form matter.

As soon as we penetrate that secret, even if lightly, we are on our way to understanding the nature of health and well-being through stillness.

"What we have called matter is energy, whose vibration has been so lowered as to be perceptible to the senses. There is no matter," states Albert Einstein[21]. We are made of energy, and everything around us is too. It's just that everything vibrates at different frequencies.

If we regard our physical bodies in this light, we can clearly see that we would be easily affected by the vibration of things and people around us.

Feeling harmonious or being in harmony with someone becomes about vibrational frequency. Even the *intention* of a vibration can alter the material world, as Dr. Masaru Emoto proved in his experiments that showed how our voice, tone, emotions, and even our thoughts can impact the way water crystalizes.

The science of cymatics[22], or vibrations, shows how sound frequencies move through water, air, or sand and change the vibration of "matter" with which they come into contact.

Taking this a step further, we might say that everything we say, feel, or think expresses a frequency that affects everything around it, like a single drop of water creates, on a still surface of water, ever-expanding ripples vibrating outward.

This would imply, then, that in our physical stillness we can experience the vibration of ourselves in harmony with ourselves and the world.

In a way, achieving stillness within our body may be described as vibrating in perfect harmony with our self. Most things cause us to vibrate disharmoniously. We notice it particularly with the effect of sound, but all our senses are affected.

Try humming when you're upset, for example, and see how your mood immediately changes. Or shake your body, shimmy, wiggle your hands and feet, then feel the stillness settling back into more harmony.

Much of my work is to try to get my clients in harmony with themselves and the world. One of the ways I do this is through music. In 1953 the International Standards Organization decided that music, internationally, should be tuned to A = 440 Hz. But this might not be the pitch that suits humans best, and may even have an unhealthy effect on our consciousness. According to some researchers, the effect on the electric potential of the brain could possibly "alter and affect memory and perception by the slight change and charge within the water in our cells."[23]

Rudolf Steiner noted that music based A=432 hz supports us on our journey toward what he termed spiritual freedom. "Music based on C=128 Hz (C not in concert 432 Hz) will support humanity on its way towards spiritual freedom. The inner ear of the human being is built on C=128 Hz." [24] This is why I use a heart sounding bowl that I tune to A = 432 hz, which vibrates in harmony with the natural resonance of nature and the cosmos.

Getting in tune with ourselves, with each other, and with the world is at the foundation of well-being.

The vibration of color affects us too. When schools are painted in bright, resonant, vibrant colors instead of the dull, dark spaces most students are used to, "attendance improves, graffiti disappears, and kids actually say they feel safer in these painted schools."[25]

Not surprisingly, the vibration of touch affects us as well, particularly with regard to the intention of that touch. The exact same touch on the shoulder may be patronizing, invasive, or tender, depending on its intention. Ripping off a bandage may be painful, but the same amount of pain is intensified if anger or meanness is involved.

This is why it is so important to know the source of what we eat. If that carrot has been lovingly grown in rich organic soil, it's going to have a different effect on us than one that is ignored, grown in depleted and chemically saturated soil, and sprayed with pesticides.

Eating food that has been loved, and drinking water that is fresh, allowing our sense of sight to be entranced by color and aesthetic beauty, listening to sounds that are in harmony with our inner ear—these are all ways that vibrate us into our own harmony, which then allows us to connect with the innate stillness within.

It is when we vibrate in concert with our own true vibration that we are still.

When we begin to vibrate in concert with the organic quiet of things being just what they are, not trying to be anything other than what they are, we become still.

Getting in Tune with Yourself

> "I love to think of nature as an unlimited
> broadcasting station, through which God speaks to
> us every hour, if we will only tune in." —George
> Washington Carver

Getting in tune with ourselves is one of the best ways to detach from the almighty 'should' that rules so much of our lives.

A while back, a friend gifted a reading with me to someone who was getting married in a few weeks.

Tiffany was a large, cheerful young woman. She bounded into my studio with a broad smile, made the usual noises of appreciation, and flopped on the couch, looking at me expectantly.

"So what does my future look like?" she asked, chirpily.

I was playing my heart sounding bowl as she spoke, syncopating the vibration of our energies. I went on playing for a while, because it was hard to tune into her.

After a while I felt that beneath her beaming, cheerful exterior was a jangling tension.

I tried to settle into relaxation, but she was full of a nervous energy. Of course, it was possible that the stress of the upcoming large wedding was beneath the tension.

But it seemed more than that. I guided her into deeper relaxation—tried to get her to breathe more rhythmically. I could see it wasn't easy.

"Why is it so hard for you to breathe?" I asked.

She replied sharply, "I've been getting panic attacks. They're normal."

"Panic attacks aren't normal," I said.

"They're not? Everyone says you get them when you're getting married."

"It's as though you're all jangled up and out of

tune. What is going on with you that keeps untuning you? You're like an instrument that keeps dropping to the ground or going off-key."

"What do you mean?" She was still sitting up straight on the couch, her hands resting awkwardly in her lap, her wide face still smiling. I could tell she did not like where this was going.

"I'm getting the sense that you're out of tune with yourself. I don't mean about your health—I mean your soul-health. What triggers your panic attacks?"

She shrugged. "Random."

I went on playing my heart sounding bowl, and eventually she began to calm down. Her cheeriness was replaced with an inward quiet.

"You want to know about your future," I spoke softly. "What is it that you want to know about?"

By this time her eyes were closed. Her voice was so low I could hardly hear her when she asked: "Should I marry my fiancé?"

She'd spoken her truth. Now I realized what was underlying the jangling, out-of-tune energy I had sensed.

"Let's take a look," I said, gently.

We created a tarot spread in the form of a crossroads, exactly where she was at the moment. One road led to the marriage that was already in the works. The other road led to not going through with the wedding.

I didn't talk much, since I realized she was facing something she had completely refused to ask herself till now. Tarot images, like dreams, can penetrate our psyche even without having an intuitive reader interpret what the cards mean.

The two roads were distinctly different and I knew I had to let her experience each one for herself. The road toward following through on the wedding and marrying her fiancé showed up with a four of pentacles and a ten of pentacles. Solid, firm, secure stability. Who wouldn't want that in a marriage?

The road toward choosing *not* to marry him showed up as an eight of swords.

"That's a card that speaks of enormous trust in the universe," I said. "You don't know where or why, but if you choose that path, you need to trust it, even when it looks hard."

The last card was the chariot. It was upside-down, and although I don't usually read reversals, I thought it was interesting how she kept turning it around and around in her hands.

"What does this mean?" she asked at last.

"It has to do with commitment. Pulling your head in the same direction as your heart. Committing to one direction—the direction of your soul's longing. The direction to your real home."

She nodded.

Then she looked again at her marriage road and I almost saw her cringe. What might appear to many people as an ideal path for getting married, felt to her claustrophobic and weighty. She saw it so clearly herself that I did not have to say anything.

She lifted her eyes to mine and I saw that hers were filled with tears.

"But he's such a nice man. He's so good."

"I know. That's why he deserves more."

She nodded again.

Even though I'd brought her face to face with the source of her panic, I could see that now she was breathing more calmly and seemed more tranquil. Her harmonious relief felt like the climax of a symphony that has meandered all over the place and then finally resolves itself into its initial key. She knew it wasn't going to be an easy time, but she also knew she wouldn't be having any more panic attacks.

Slow Down into Stillness

"Sometimes the fastest way to grow is to slow down." —Stewart Blackburn

One of the best ways to touch, light up, and activate your inner stillness is to slow down.

Try this: let your purpose in doing anything be the activity itself. Read a book more slowly. Appreciate each interesting phrase. Look up some words you're unfamiliar with.

Give yourself more time to drive to work and take a different route.

Allow an hour or two to prepare a meal and enjoy the entire process rather than the meal itself.

Eat more slowly—savor what you drink by sipping and consciously experiencing the myriad tastes.

Going slow is about loving what you're doing and being loved by it. Become intimate with your activity—savor it—treat it like a lover. You'll be amazed how it reciprocates with peaceful, healing stillness.

One of my clients was a well-known chef and restauranteur. Before owning his popular restaurant, Dennis had been creating a successful business and brand for himself as a world-class chef, specializing in using locally grown food.

When I met him, he seemed larger-than-life—a bestselling author and an internationally acclaimed celebrity. He was also passionate and precise about everything he did and said. He spoke firmly and with authority. His large arms were folded as he leaned slightly back, gazing down at me as though from a great height.

I was honored to meet him, having delighted in his books and some of his vegetarian recipes. I knew him to be a witty, sarcastic, and brilliant human being.

He wasn't the sort of client with whom I could enter into a meditation right away. He restlessly studied the books on my shelves and picked up some of the healing crystals I'd laid out. He asked questions about some of the objects and made a comment about my numerous tarot decks.

He didn't seem to want to go into the peaceful sacred space that many of my clients seek when they come to see me: He wanted answers and he wanted them right away.

I settled him on the couch and brought him to a state of quiet and receptivity through a brief guided visualization. His eyes closed.

We sat in silence for a few minutes, then he asked
the question that I knew was at the heart of the
matter:

Why aren't I happy?

He didn't tell me anything about himself. He
didn't want to answer my questions about what he
loved to do when he was five years old or if he was in
a relationship.

"That's not what it's about," he stated, firmly and
authoritatively.

Briefly, I considered the possibility that I might
not be able to help him. I work best when my client
trusts me, knows I'm here to help, and doesn't mind
opening up a little so I can do that in the best way I
know how.

But I liked him, admired him, and the issue of
happiness is one that is dear to my heart. I've studied
it for many years, read many books on the subject,
explored the research, and talked about it with many
people. So I drew out my tarot deck and said,
reassuringly and confidently, "Okay then, let's take a
look. What does Dennis need to do in order to be
happy?"

I laid out the cards like a relationship: Dennis on
the left, Happiness on the right, and above them,
completing the triangle, the relationship between the

two as it currently existed. It seemed a logical, helpful window into seeing what was going on.

I had a feeling we would understand all we needed to know from the wisdom of the three cards, but we still had an hour ahead of us, so I laid out four more cards, face down. The first, to left of the card that represented Dennis: "What you need to leave behind." The second, underneath the Dennis card, "Your plan of action, your strategy." The third, to the right of the card that represented his Happiness: "What Happiness would like you to know about it." And the fourth, "The potential for you to feel the synthesis between you and Happiness." I added that card represented something close to "the future," but told him to keep in mind that the future is only potential until it happens.

As he gazed at the green-and-gold backs of the deck, I could tell he was intrigued, wondering what would be revealed.

I turned over the Dennis card first. "This is you, as you are now in your relationship to Happiness," I reminded him.

Not surprisingly, it was the Ten of Swords, a man lying face down in a pool of blood with ten swords plunged into his back. Dennis recoiled, laughed nervously, then picked up the card and forced himself look at it.

"You're exhausted," I said matter-of-factly. "It's as though you're wearing a huge, heavy winter overcoat on the hottest of summer days. *Of course* you're feeling miserable. But you don't have to be." I pointed out that if he looked beyond all those swords on the card he would see the dawning of a new day in the background.

He nodded, replacing the card, but didn't say anything.

"No one can be happy when they're wearing a thick, heavy coat on a hot day," I said. "You'll need to take it off and leave it behind. It's become like a corpse ... why would you want to carry a corpse around with you?"

"What do you mean?"

"You're carrying around old stuff ... ways of living that don't fit you any more or don't suit you. Or perhaps these are thoughts or weighty feelings?" When he didn't answer, I said, "Well, we'll have to see then."

I turned over the Happiness card: the Hermit.

"What does that mean?" he asked, picking it up.

"Go inward—know thyself. Your happiness is inside you, not outside. It's time to explore it, to learn about it. You think it's something you can go after and find. You think it's something that's eluding you. But it's inside you and it's something you can know and experience rather than seek."

He shrugged. "Okay, may as well go on."

The card representing the relationship between Dennis and Happiness was the Ace of Swords.

"A new perspective—you do need to see happiness differently than you do now." I gazed at the eagle in the clouds and the sword that pierced through to the sky. I heard myself say: "There is a completely new way ahead for you—you *can* be happy. But it's not in any way you can imagine right now." I looked up at him. "Are you depressed?"

"Supposedly," he replied briefly.

"You don't have to be," I smiled at him. "You'll be all right."

We turned over the card representing what he needed to leave behind: the Seven of Wands, a card I often consider one the most personal and spiritual of all the cards. The energy of Jacob wrestling with the Angel swelled in the room like a symphony. I felt it had been a long, dark night for Dennis.

"Leave behind the wrestling with your soul. Leave behind wondering why you're doing what you're doing, why you are who you are, and what life is all about. Let it be. Let the stillness show you the way."

"Sure," he said, sarcastically, fidgeting, but holding my gaze instead of looking at the cards.

I smiled encouragingly. "You're doing great already," I said. "Ready for your action plan?"

Although he was sarcastic and cynical, he had a curious, interested light in his expression when I asked this. An unidentifiable positive energy filled the room. We gazed at each other, but neither of us spoke.

I turned my gaze and showed him his action plan: the Hanged Man, swinging calmly in the breeze.

"Well, that doesn't look good," he pronounced, choking on a laugh.

"He *is* good," I protested, for the Hanged Man is one of my dearest friends in the tarot. "I told you, you need a different perspective. There it is."

He turned it around, as though it were a hand on a clock, and I heard a voice in my ear, as clear as a tick-tock sound: *Slow down. Slow down. Slow down.*

"You'll feel happiness when you slow down," I stated. "The hanged man is telling you to stop chasing after everything you think you need to chase after, and to surrender to whatever is in the moment."

"Yeah, 'live in the present.' Sure." He rolled his eyes at the cliché of it.

"This goes beyond mere mindfulness," I went on, still hearing the 'slow down—slow down' in my ear. "You can't be mindful without slowing down."

"I can't slow down."

"Let's see what Happiness wants you to know about it." I turned over the Ten of Cups. A rainbow lightly touched the roof of a cozy house. "It's waiting for you. How does this card make you feel?"

"It looks nice. Not possible, though."

"It *is* possible. Slow down. Let go."

"Well, I can't let go of my business," he said, but his voice was not as forceful as it had been.

"Why not?" I asked.

He gave a startled jump. "It's who I am."

I laughed out loud. "It certainly is not! Maybe it's part of who you are—a small part."

He had never considered this before.

I pressed my advantage: "You were the spirit of Dennis before you were born, and you were Dennis at age three and five, and when you were in school --- and you'll still be Dennis whether or not you cook or write or no one ever hears of you again. And you'll be the spirit of Dennis after you die, and then you'll be reborn, maybe, and likely as not it won't be as a chef."

He let out a big, hearty laugh.

"Okay, so how do I slow down?" he asked. "I've never done that before."

"Why don't you begin by slowing down just one thing—maybe just how you drink your cup of coffee in the morning. Savor it, sip it more slowly. Stir your spoon clockwise, slowly, then counter-clockwise even more slowly. Notice. Be with it. Smell it."

"I don't take anything in my coffee so I don't need a spoon."

"All the better. You'll be stirring your coffee slowly as a meditation, not for any other reason. Then taste it—really taste it."

"Yes, sometimes I feel as though I've forgotten how to taste—it's all about having to get the damned food on the table or the video filmed right. Everything's on a tight schedule. But I do take vacations."

"I bet your vacations are *not* about slowing down." I did know a bit about what he did on his celebrity-paced vacations, so I knew I was right. "How about renting a little seaside cottage on an island, far from anyone you know, and just lying in a hammock for a month."

He laughed out loud again and I joined in.

"No, seriously," I persisted.

"I can't. A *month*? No way."

"Yes, you can."

"I've got obligations, responsibilities, a career."

I could see that he wasn't sure whether I knew he was famous.

"I know. I'm not talking about that, though—I'm answering your question about why you're not happy. You're not letting yourself be happy. You're so wrapped up in shoulds and have-tos and deadlines, and your preconception that success and happiness have something to do with each other, that you've forgotten your real self."

"You see an island in my future?"

I sighed, wondering if he'd heard a word I'd said. "It's up to you how far you want to go with this, how important not being depressed is, and how much happiness means to you. But you can certainly feel happy if you want to."

Our time was up and I was saddened by the possibility that I hadn't been able to help him more. Before he left I gave him a small piece of smoky quartz that I carried in my purse.

"Keep it in your pocket, if you'd like to," I told him. "Whenever you need to be reminded to slow down, there it will be. We'll call it your slow-down crystal."

It was the best I could do. He left and I wondered

whether I'd ever see him again.

To my delight, a year after our first meeting Dennis contacted me. And we've met annually since then. It's taken him five years to slowly extricate himself from the jaws of a life that was so strenuously busy he'd lost any ability to enjoy it. Through the steady practice of slowing down, little by little he'd shed one aspect of his business after another. He moved to Hawai'i to work in an already-established restaurant there. He's fallen off the radar of celebrity chefs, but he's married, has a young child, and is learning to surf.

And, yes, he says he's happy.

Be in Nature

> *"My heart is tuned to the quietness that the stillness of nature inspires." —Hazrat Inayat Khan*

One of the best, most pleasurable ways to vibrate in harmony with ourselves—so that we reach a state of stillness—is being in nature. Nature herself is a great healer.

When we're surrounded by the natural world, our bodies and minds relax and we begin to feel better.

For many people, being in nature, whether hiking, gardening, or lying in a hammock, may be more conducive to stillness than being in a room and focusing on trying to be still.

I have spent much of my life in nature, but its power and reciprocal healing aspect was brought to consciousness during a quiet experience of *shinrin-yoku*, the Japanese practice of forest bathing, led by forest therapy expert Annabel O'Neill.[26]

I signed up for one of Annabel's forest therapy walks taking place one afternoon in late spring. Five of us walked through the misty rain into the heart of a wooded area and stood in a circle. None of us had done anything like this before.

Annabel told us that she would be giving us a short practices to reflect on, then we'd go off on our own, rejoin the circle after fifteen minutes or so, and share our experiences.

The first practice was to "notice something you've never noticed before." We all went in separate directions to have our individual experiences. I clambered through some shrubbery, following the sound of a stream. Through the wet green leaves, I glimpsed a purple-blue color and, drawn by it, I found myself in a small clearing that was thickly covered with fragrant violets.

I sat on a mossy fallen log and looked around. The stream was to my right, down a sloping hill. Violets grew wherever I looked. The rain was hardly perceptible under the mantle of fresh, new leaves overhead.

I was transported, vividly and quickly, into my adolescence in Sussex. There was no distinct or particular memory, just the feeling of rain and springtime that made the memory seem utterly visceral and real.

Then I became aware of the scent of violets. Our sense of smell is probably the oldest of our five primary senses, and associated most strongly with memory and emotion. It occurred to me, as I sat there, that just as I sometimes use music to allow stillness, so I could use fragrance. Perhaps I would use the essential oil of violet to correlate with stillness. If I used it regularly, I figured I'd establish a relationship between the fragrance of violets and stillness.

(It has worked supremely well. When I'm feeling particularly hurried or unsettled, or don't have a lot of time, the fragrance works on my subconscious and takes me to a place of stillness in an instant.)

The research that has gone into *shinrin-yoku* has

shown the profound benefits of being in nature, including lowering blood pressure, blood glucose levels, and stress hormones.[27] During the meditative practice of forest bathing, we are not mulling a conundrum at work or what to cook for dinner. Instead, we become consciously aware of what is around us. As Eckhart Tolle writes in *Stillness Speaks*:

> To bring your attention to a stone, a tree, or an animal does not mean to think about it, but simply to perceive it, to hold it in your awareness. Something of its essence then transmits itself to you. You can sense how still it is, and in doing so the same stillness arises within you. You sense how deeply it rests in Being — completely at one with what it is and where it is. In realizing this, you to come to a place of rest deep within yourself.[28]

Fifteen minutes into my violet experience, I heard Annabel's low whistle calling us back to the circle. We all had various stories to share, but the one that struck me the most that afternoon was from Mary:

"Last week a wild animal — probably a squirrel — got trapped in my garage. It created lots of damage, tore apart some of the wall, knocked over things, and my car was scratched. I felt really angry and annoyed. But this afternoon I suddenly saw the experience from the point of view of the squirrel — it had gotten trapped in a strange place and must have been terrified. I felt a new compassion for it and wished I hadn't been so annoyed and instead more helpful. It was just being a squirrel."

Nature teaches compassion, because it models for us that we don't have to be anything other than our true nature. When we see ourselves or others as they are, we don't judge or criticize. Do we criticize a flame for being hot or snow for being cold? It is being what it is, expressing its true nature.

As German philosopher Martin Heidegger describes it, existence has to do with understanding one's own nature and purpose.[29] Since nature exists purely for itself, and it understands that its purpose is to be itself and to become itself, it is a tremendously powerful teacher for us.

It shows us that our purpose is the same: to be ourselves and to become ourselves.

What I was realized most from my forest therapy experience was that being in nature and with nature, mindfully and in stillness, is profoundly healing, inspiring, and freeing, because we are reminded that all that is being asked of us in this life is to be and to become who we truly are.

The Art of Surrender

> *"Always say 'yes' to the present moment...*
> *Surrender to what is." –Eckhart Tolle*

The secret to thoroughly experiencing physical stillness is through the act of surrender. Craniosacral master and author Charles Ridley calls it "allowance." In the physical body, through allowing stillness to occur, wellness happens naturally.

I've seen this happen through a gentle, reminding touch on the shoulder. Or when I let myself be permeated by the sound of intense, rhythmic shamanic drumming or in that marvelous hypnagogic state between sleeping and waking when I can be completely relaxed.

It's not about searching for stillness: it is *surrendering* to it.

Just as a flower surrenders to its fragrance, or a bird surrenders to its song, we can surrender gently to what is around in nature—from the magnificent sky to the tiniest flower—and experience the stillness that occurs within ourselves. Eckart Tolle says: "We have forgotten what rocks, plants, and animals still know. We have forgotten how to be—to be still, to be ourselves, to be where life is. Here and now."[30]

Surrendering to stillness is the key to wellness. When we invite the allowing of stillness in ourselves, and to welcome, trust, nurture it, the power of stillness creates space for healing.

One day I was scheduled to meet with a client at three o'clock on a Friday afternoon, late in September. I'd worked with her a few times before, so I felt prepared and ready when a car pulled into my driveway. But the woman who got out was not my client but a stranger. She was small and delicate, and it was hard to tell her age. Her dark clothes were baggy on her thin frame. I greeted her and asked where my client was. She looked surprised and told me her friend had offered to gift her this session instead. Hadn't she told me?

No, she hadn't. Not knowing anything about this new client, nor why she was there, felt disconcerting. But I invited her into my healing studio and gave her a glass of water, which she drank gratefully. She told me her name was Natalie and I asked her to lie down on my couch. I sensed she needed tenderness, so I made her feel as cozy as possible, tucking a soft blanket around her. Immediately, she closed her eyes and I almost thought she'd gone right to sleep.

"Thank you," Natalie murmured.

With the help of my meditation sounding bowl and soothing words, I lulled her into a sweet, childlike land of calm, dreamlike colors and peacefulness. Her breathing became more and more even, and I could tell she was close to sleep, which would not necessarily be helpful. So I asked her why she had wanted to come to see me.

Her eyes remained closed.

"My beautiful fifteen-year-old daughter was killed in a car accident last month," she pronounced. Her voice was pragmatic and strong, as though she'd spoken this sentence over and over in an effort to make herself believe it. "I want to connect with her. I want to know that she's all right."

The awful sadness struck me like a hard blow to my chest. As her words sank in, I felt utterly helpless.

I can't help her! I cried inwardly. This was an impossible task! How could I guide her through the worst nightmare imaginable?

It is at moments like these that I feel I am out of my depth in the work I am called to do. How can anything I say or do in any way lift Natalie's immense cloud of grief and sorrow? Who was I to touch the sacred land of this much grief?

In our day-to-day encounters with people who are suffering we can express our compassion, or sorrow, or give advice (usually unsolicited), or offer a hug. In a setting like the one I create for my clients, I can do none of those things. I did not want to react ("Oh, dear, I'm so sorry!") or burst into tears (which I was close to doing), or give advice. Natalie was not asking for advice.

But she *was* asking for my help, and so I needed to help her.

At the same time, I did not know how.

I went on playing my meditation sounding bowl and silently asking for help. I could not do this alone, I reminded the angels and any other helpful energies that were present. *Help me to help her.* I tried to garner all the stillness in my heart that I could muster. What could I say? If only I'd known ahead of time I could have thought about words to say!

It was a beautiful fall day, and the sun streamed in through the windows as though from a pure, angelic light. I let the warm light calm me. When I can become still, everything becomes imbued with a clarity that is beyond mere sunshine. Even the song of a robin right outside my window sounded purer and sweeter than usual.

The candle I'd lit flickered in front of me and I remembered the wisest lesson that stillness had taught me: *There's nothing you have to do. You have to be. Just allow.*

In that moment I was humbled to the core of my being. Of course there was nothing I could say or do to help this grieving mother go on with her life. No one can. It's not possible.

But this wasn't about me.

And I *could* channel help from angels, from Source, and from her daughter. I could exist as a small little conduit that allowed love and courage to flow into this woman's heart and soul.

I could get out of the way. I could let Love to do its own work.

I have no recollection of what was said during that hour we shared together. All I know is that I felt a streaming energy of overflowing love filling up the space within us and all around us, and Natalie was feeling it too.

Natalie did not need to be told her daughter was alright, safe and beloved, in her spiritual adventure where she was now. She needed to *feel* it. And that was what I needed to give her space for.

Before she left, she hugged me hard. "Can I see you again?" she asked. "You've given me so many ideas of how my family and I might be able to move forward."

I smiled, because I knew I hadn't given her any ideas—they had all come from within herself. I found out during the many following sessions we had together, that she was clearly seeing guideposts that she could use to take her into her future. She heard directions and encouragement that helped her live her own life, even without her daughter being with her on this planet. I'm not a traditional medium, but her daughter's presence is intensely real to me whenever I'm with her mother. Sometimes I feel I'm hosting a little tea party for the two of them to be together.

In the beginning Natalie wanted to go on seeing me because that feeling of being with her daughter was so very sweet to her. Eventually, she returned because she saw how she could rebuild her trust in life. She could repair a damaged relationship with her husband, focus on her career, and live again. There was still lots for her to accomplish, ways for her to grow, and even to enjoy.

She had thought her life had come to a complete standstill when the call had come about her daughter's death. But she realized that although it was a terrible pause in her life, it was not the end.

Be Playful

> *I met a Puppy as I went walking;*
> *We got talking,*
> *Puppy and I.*
> *"Where are you going this nice fine day?"*
> *(I said to the Puppy as he went by).*
> *"Up to the hills to roll and play."*
> *"I'll come with you, Puppy," said I.*
> --A.A.Milne

One of my favorite poems growing up was A. A. Milne's 'Puppy and I,' about a young child encountering various beings (a Man, a Horse, a Woman, a Rabbit) who are busy with their have-to work tasks and errands. Each one invites the child to accompany them, but he declines.

It's only when he meets a puppy, whose delightful plan for the day is to go up to the hills to roll and play, that the child accepts the invitation to go along.

Imagine if instead of play time being scheduled and squeezed around the more 'important' work of academic classes or making a monetary living or doing errands, the reverse were true: Play time is our central rhythm, and in between we spent a bit of time working.

We need to listen to that invitation of our hearts

to roll and play in the hills as often as we can, in
whatever way that means to us—because play, too, is
stillness.

Air — Stillness in the Mental Body

*"To the mind that is still, the whole universe
surrenders."* —*Lao Tzu*

Imagine our beautiful planet Earth as a body that breathes. All around her is an atmosphere that we know as air. Air is the clear gas (mostly a mixture of nitrogen and oxygen) in which living things exist and breathe. Air has no shape, no volume, no color, no smell. It is physically real, however, since it does have measurable mass and weight.

Our incessant respiration is the activity of breathing air. The word *respiration* originates from the Latin word *spiritus*: breathing, respiration, the wind, breath of a god, and breath of life. In other words, it animates our spirit.

It is also physical: we breathe in the oxygen that is in the air, our lungs share the oxygen with our blood, and then our outbreath sends carbon dioxide to the air, which plants need to live.

What this means is that we all need each other. We are breathing together, in a symbiotic, rhythmic inhaling and exhaling throughout our physical existence on this planet.

Air Pollution

> *"Take a course in good water and air; and in the eternal youth of Nature you may renew your own. Go quietly, alone; no harm will befall you." – John Muir*

While air is mostly gas, it also holds miniscule particles of dust, pollen, and other bits and pieces of our atmosphere. Things like pollen are crucial to our human existence, since they spread the plant forms we need to create oxygen.

But air can also carry other particles, impurities like exhaust, ash, and smoke, which are damaging to our health, the health of all interconnected beings of the planet, and the planet itself.

Thought Pollution

> *"Thoughts are like the breeze or the leaves on the trees or the raindrops falling. They appear like that, and through inquiry we can make friends with them. Would you argue with a raindrop? Raindrops aren't personal, and neither are thoughts."* – Byron Katie

Our thoughts have a similar problem. We need the clarity and objective awareness that thinking enables in us in order to grow and evolve. But our mental health is easily polluted by thoughts that clutter, traumatize, or hinder us from moving freely in our essential nature.

The pollution we experience in our minds tends to happen when we confuse our thoughts with our feelings. We say things like "I feel worried" or "I feel guilty" or "I feel anxious" or "I feel stressed."

But each of those phrases is a thought, *not a feeling.* That is, they are not a feeling until we invite our thought inside, attach to it, take it seriously, and allow it to take over our psyche.

When we let our thoughts float through us, and we don't attach to them, we find that they carry no emotion whatsoever.

Think about it: Thoughts are neutral and have no energy of their own. Our thoughts help us to understand and frame things objectively. Our innate intelligence becomes available through thought. Thinking is a great skill and a wonderful tool that helps us survive and thrive.

But when we hold onto our thoughts too tightly, they become at best distracting and at worst debilitating. If we let it, a thought may produce anxiety, guilt, shame, and worry, and extend into depression, or behavioral and emotional problems; these can then surface as relationship challenges, professional stuckness, or even diagnosed personality disorders.

Becoming attached to our thoughts can become a relentless habit. Thich Nhat Hanh describes this as "Radio NST" (Non-Stop Thinking). "Cows, goats, and buffalo chew their food, swallow it, then regurgitate and rechew it multiple times," he writes. "We may not be cows or buffalo, but we ruminate just the same on our thoughts—unfortunately, primarily negative thoughts. We eat them, and then we bring them up to chew again and again, like a cow chewing its cud."[31]

When we hold on to a thought, and begin chewing it, we give it way too much power. We lose sight of the neutrality of that thought. A thought, in and of itself, has no energy or validity, much less emotion.

Byron Katie writes in her groundbreaking book called *Loving What Is – Four Questions that Can Change Your Life*: "A thought is harmless unless we believe it. It's not our thoughts, but the attachment to our thoughts, that causes suffering. Attaching to a thought means believing that it's true, without inquiring. A belief is a thought that we've been attaching to, often for years."[32]

Everyone suffers, to some extent, and all our suffering originates in our thinking. By this point we don't even realize we are suffering—we think it's just a natural part of being human.[33] We think it's normal. But it's not. It is the attachment to the thought that makes us believe we are suffering. We can change our thinking even about a thought, by detaching from it.

This insight has been posited by holistic and metaphysical practitioners, poets, mystics, and philosophers for centuries, including the seventeenth-century poet John Milton, who wrote the following lines in *Paradise Lost*:

> The mind is its own place, and in itself
> Can make a Heaven of Hell, a Hell of Heaven.

If we can allow thoughts to move through us and past us, we release the feelings that the thoughts engender. For example, when we let thoughts of judgment, resentment, anger, and bitterness to pass through us without attaching to them, we experience a feeling of well-being—our suffering ceases and we are at peace. We open to the possibilities that live beyond mental chatter. We not only feel better, but we can become imaginative, creative, and joyful. But how do we do this?

Stillness is the key. In stillness, we learn how to release our thoughts, and let them float freely through our minds, without getting caught up in them or turning them into worry, fear, guilt, and anxiety. Like a wild bird, a thought can get out of control when it's trapped in our psyche, creating chaos and even damage. But when it is gently coaxed and released, it remains benign. It has no connection to us except as something to be impartially observed.

The Art of Commitment

"You need to make a commitment, and once you make it, then life will give you some answers." –Les Brown

John was a thirty-nine-year-old filmmaker who traveled frequently between Atlanta, New York, and Los Angeles for his career. When he came to see me, his question seemed straightforward enough: "Where is the best place for me to live so that my career's the most successful?"

Of course, anyone who knows the film industry would advise him to move straight back to Los Angeles—the Mecca of filmmaking—and do whatever it takes to be successful. But as he told me a little about his work, I could see him turning over the pros and cons of moving to this place over that place in his head. It was clear that it was a confusing, tiring, and joyless process. The energy of thinking is wonderful when it's clear and decisive, but when it gets trapped it can be incapacitating.

I wondered why this decision was so hard for him. First I asked why he currently lived in Atlanta? He told me he'd had steady work there for an ongoing television film project and he liked it there.

But he added that he'd never be as successful as he wanted to be if he stayed there.

Then why, I wondered, was Los Angeles even up for debate? And why was he so restless? Why did he keep moving from one city to the next? Was it a creative project he needed to work on or a career strategy? Or was it something else?

When I asked him, he didn't seem to know. Why had he left Los Angeles in the first place? He shrugged helplessly. But the more we talked about it, the more confused he seemed to get.

As I turned over some tarot cards for him, I sensed profound feminine challenges rising up, not so much in him, but in regard to women in his life. I turned over a Queen of Cups, then a Queen of Swords, they stood shoulder to shoulder and stared at him balefully.

He looked a bit startled when I asked him about his mother. His square-jawed, slightly unshaven face seemed closed and his mouth hardened. He told me he hardly ever spoke with her.

"She's the most narcissistic person I know," he said coldly.

"Los Angeles was not where he needed to be just now?" I asked.

"Exactly."

His voice was abrupt—he didn't want to discuss her.

"Do you have siblings?" I asked.

"A sister—a year younger than me. We lived together for a while when we were in LA. Then she wanted to move to London. She's a dancer."

There was both affection and hurt in his voice. I could feel their energies tightly entwined like snakes coiled together... neither negative nor positive, but perhaps too tightly entwined. Intuitively, I could tell that they were holding onto cellular memories of having to protect each other through a childhood that was too painful to endure without each other's support.

So now I knew that before we could explore the question of where he should settle, we had to gently and imaginatively extricate his mother and sister from the decision. I helped him do this by reminding him that he was not responsible for either of them. His relationship with his mother was complete—he needed to set her—and himself—free. As long as he harbored bitterness or anger toward her, he wasn't going be able to move on with his own life.

I got out my rattle and began rattling around his various chakras, trying to release the energy that had gotten so stuck between mother and son, reminding him that freedom can only come through gratitude, appreciation, and love—not through anger or resentment.

When I heard him finally laughing out loud at some of the positive words I was using about his mother, saying how wonderful it was that he was born, and how hard she tried in spite of herself, and how free he was now that he was a grown-up and wise, I put away the rattle.

"Now, your sister," I said.

"She's in London now," he answered, looking much more relaxed. "She says she's going to stay there for now. I can't believe it."

"Why can't you believe it?"

"It's so far away. She doesn't know what she's doing."

"What do you mean?"

"She's not good at taking care of herself. Paying bills, practical things, you know? How will she manage?"

"Let her try," I advised. "You might be surprised."

"Yes, I probably think I need to take care of her. She thinks I'm always criticizing her."

"You don't need to take care of her. I mean, you do, but in a different way than you've been doing.

You need to take care of the love you have for each other. But you also need to trust her to make her own decisions. You need to let her be herself."

He sighed. "My therapist's told me that too."

"Try saying it out loud to your sister, even if you don't feel it yourself yet. Try telling her that you absolutely trust her to make the best decisions for herself and her life, and that she has your unconditional, loving support for anything she does or will do."

He laughed again. "Okay, I'll try."

I told him what a good sport he was, and then I shuffled the tarot cards again. I often find that accessing the stillness of the air element—the mental body—can create the quickest shift for clients. Through the rattle, John's repetitive thinking patterns had been dispersed and his confusion lifted. My words had turned his perspective upside down and made him laugh. His mental, trapped energy had shifted.

"Now we can find out where you need to live," I stated.

I laid out four cards: one card for him, and then three cards above him: New York, Los Angeles, and Atlanta. I turned over his significator card—the card that represented him. It was the Knight of Wands, so I had a strong feeling he'd be moving soon.

That meant we didn't need to spend much time on the possibility of his staying on in Atlanta. So I turned that card over: it was the Ten of Wands...an ending. A completion. Yes, it was definitely time for a move, a new start.

As I had set down each card, I had assumed that Los Angeles would show up as his future destiny. But, instead, the card in the Los Angeles position revealed itself as the Tower. The Tower often shows up as a powerful warning. It's not bad or good—it just is. In fact, none of the energies of the tarot cards are bad or good—they are all neutral, and helpful, guides. But, just as energy can get blocked and create trauma or sickness, and like water can become blocked and thus get stagnant, the Tower may show up at a time when it's important to move through something that otherwise would hold you back from your destiny.

Now I felt its thunder-and-lightning energy loomed with intense advice: *Clear away all those old ways of thinking! Don't get stuck in the past! Your foundation is strong but this structure is not where you need to be. Don't get caught up in the shoulds and have-tos just for the sake of your film career.*

I saw at once that Los Angeles was not where he needed to be just now. I had no idea why that would be so, given that he was a committed and successful filmmaker, but that was what the energy was telling us.

He picked up the card and studied it. "Does this card mean there's going to be an earthquake in LA?" he grinned, sardonically.

"It's a symbol of the earthquake that would happen in your life if you moved there. You'd be living out something that's already behind you. You wouldn't be happy, even if you were successful. Why not? I don't know. Okay, now let's look at New York." And I turned over that card.

And there before us was the beautiful Lovers card, beaming a passionate guiding light in the direction of New York. The Lovers card is not necessarily about romantic love, but it is about choosing what you love, or, at the very least, choosing wisely and committing to that choice.

In this particular instance, however, I was struck by the conviction that in New York he would find his romantic partner. Cautiously, I drew another card for New York to see if my sense of romance was on the right track. Galloping ardently toward us was the Knight of Cups, holding in his hands a cup that contained the most romantic energy in the entire deck.

"So, my dear," I informed him, "your question is not about where you ought to live in order to ensure you have a successful career. Your question is about love, romance, marriage, commitment. And that question can only be answered by your moving to New York."

His gray-green eyes were fastened musingly on the two cards in front of him, the Lovers and the Knight of Cups.

I asked him about his love life. "Are you in love? Engaged? Married?"

"I just had my heart broken," he said slowly.

"No, you haven't," I smiled. "Your heart is fine."

He still didn't look at me. "You're right," he said, still slowly. He seemed bewildered by what the cards were revealing to him.

"New York is where your lover waits," I stated. "Your question isn't about your career—you'll be successful wherever you go. That's just who you are. But love is more important right now."

He nodded. And then he said, as though he could hardly believe what he was seeing in the cards, "I know. And I even know who the person is. I thought I couldn't commit to New York because maybe LA was better for my career. But if I committed to living in New York, then I'd also be committing to her. I see that now."

"So your question is not about where to live but who to love. And here's your answer: Love the one who loves you best. All you need to do is decide, today, that you're going back to New York. You'll feel as though you've waved a magic wand simply by deciding. Create magic, happiness, and clarity by making the decision. In this single hour, you've ensured both your film success *and* true love."

He shook himself, as though to rouse himself from the amazement that clarity can shock us into sometimes. "It's so strange," he said, "I always knew I'd go back to New York. I knew I wanted to move back there again. I just wasn't sure if it was the right decision."

"You can make it the right decision," I said, "by deciding it is, right now, and committing to it."

Fear of Change

> *"Yesterday I was clever, so I wanted to change the*
> *world. Today I am wise, so I am changing myself."*
> —*Rumi*

One of the most persistent thoughts that can wreak havoc in our psyche has to do with our fear of change. Fear of change is innate in humans—the fear that change is coming and that the change may make things worse than they are now.

For the most part, the effects of change are positivity and growth, but we tend to dread it, especially when we face the changes of old age, sickness, and death.

But any fear, including fear of change, is a thought. Yes, things do keep changing throughout our lives. The very act of living implies change. And while things do change, it is also true that some things remain the same. For example, in abstract terms, we know the numbers two plus two will always add up to four and that the area of a circle will always be pi times the radius squared.[34]

Also, the fact that something has occurred will never change. Rick Hanson writes about this in his article about the healing power of stillness in an article in *Psychology Today*: "Whatever is fundamentally true—including, ironically, the truth of impermanence—has an unchanging stillness at its heart. Things change, but the *nature* of things—emergent, interdependent, transient—does not."[35]

Even when a spouse dies after a half-century of being with her partner, the upheaval and enormous change can feel potentially terrifying for the one left behind. By remembering that most of your life together has not altered at all, you can feel a renewal of hope. What has *not* changed when a loved one dies? All the many experiences that were shared, a warm, abiding love, perhaps children ...

To feel the unchanging stillness at its heart can be immensely helpful in quieting the relentless mind chatter. Here's how Hanson describes it:

> In stillness you can find a refuge, an island in the stream of changes, a place to stand for perspective and wisdom about events and your reactions to them, a respite from the race, quiet amidst the noise. Perhaps even find a sense of something transcendental, outside the frame of passing phenomena.[36]

In other words, by changing your *thought* about your fear of change, you can change your life!

When a thought is allowed to move through our mind like a cloud moving across the sky, we are left feeling serene and calm and knowing that we can handle any cloud, any rain, any storm.

The I-Ching

> Keeping still:
> *Keeping his back still*
> *So that he no longer feels his body.*
> *He goes into his courtyard*
> *And does not see his people.*
> *No blame.*
> —*I-Ching*

The ancient Chinese method of divination called the *I-Ching*, or *Book of Changes*, is based on sixty-four hexagrams that can be used for wisdom, advice, moral guidance, and as an oracle.

No one knows where the I-Ching originated. Legend has it that the dragon-human king Fu Xi was the originator of the text, which was revealed to him in the movement and changes that occur in the natural world, the animals, plants, weather, elements, and the cosmos. He translated his knowledge into eight trigrams: heaven, lake, fire, thunder, wind, water, mountain, and earth. These eight trigrams exquisitely describe the duality of our human existence: yin and yang, light and dark, masculine and feminine, dynamic and magnetic, creative and receptive. They also include the notion of 'qi,' or energy, and its constant movement and change.

I don't use the I-Ching often, but sometimes I'm drawn to its insights for a particular situation that calls for balance or when the person in front of me gives me a litany of health problems that speak to me of blocked energy.

A client came to me because she was experiencing terrible back pain and wanted my advice concerning the surgery that her doctor was recommending. Having suffered myself from excruciating back pain in the past, and finding my miracle cure through reading Dr. John Sarno's book, *Healing Back Pain*[37], I asked her first about her life situation.

She told me her husband had died a couple of years before, and she was bitter about the many years of caretaking that led up to his death. As our conversation progressed, her jaw rigid with pain, the dark circles under her eyes purple as though with bruises, she revealed more to me. It turned out that her bitterness was not as much about having to take care of her husband, but that she was hurt that her children had not been there to help out more or support her financially. They had their own families, busy careers, and two of them lived far away. Even worse, she did not get along with the sole daughter who lived nearby.

As she spoke, however, she kept dismissing her

feelings. She would defend her children for not being available, and she would blame herself for her daughter not liking her.

"I totally understand that they couldn't be there for me. My son and his wife are both lawyers and live in Seattle and they couldn't keep flying to the East Coast every time my husband fell or I needed a break."

"What's going on with the daughter that lives near you now?" I asked her.

She shook her head, but it looked to me more like a shudder. "We're always fighting," she said, grimly.

"About what?"

She swallowed, gulped, hardly able to speak the issue out loud. "She wants me to move out of my house," she said, "and go into an assisted living facility. It's just her own selfishness. She thinks she would have to take care of me if I stay where I am. I tell her she doesn't. But she thinks *I'm* being selfish."

"You sound angry," I stated, because she was beginning to sink into an energy of hopelessness and despair.

She perked up. "I *am* angry!" she exclaimed. "We can't be on the phone for five minutes before I hear myself screaming at her. Then she screams back. It's just terrible. And I hate myself for talking to my own daughter like that. The things we say to each other!"

I closed my eyes, because I hadn't forgotten her initial question when she came to me for a consultation: "Should I have the back surgery that my doctor recommends?"

Even without casting the oracle to get help from the I-Ching, the hexagram of "Keeping Still" came flooding into my mind's eye. "Keeping Still" is made up of two repeated trigrams: Ken, the Mountain, is both above and below. I could practically see the solid, quiet, grounded Mountain all around us. It was almost as though we were inside it.

"Keeping Still" describes the subtle movement between keeping still and movement without movement. One interpretation of the hexagram has to do with the egolessness of stillness. We are asked to keep our back still, because that's where the fibers that are central to movement exist. "If the movement of these spinal nerves is brought to a standstill," translator and theologian Richard Wilhelm writes, "the ego, with its restlessness, disappears."[38]

When we are calm and still, we no longer get caught up in the struggle and tumult of the environment or people around us. Well-being and true peace of mind come when we get back in harmony with the laws of the universe, with the ebb and flow, with the constant changes that occur.

Yes, the hexagram was reminding me: Change is the force of life. *Be still when it is time to be still and act when it is time to act.*

"Your back is not the issue here," I said to my client. "I can't answer your question about surgery, because you need to address something far more important first."

She looked at me questioningly, but I could tell she thought I was going to give her a homily about getting along with her family. Instead I stated firmly: "You have to face the fact that you are afraid."

She looked startled and defensive. "Afraid of what?"

"Of a lot of things. You're absolutely terrified. You're afraid you might have to rely on your daughter for help. You're afraid of moving somewhere new. You're afraid of an assisted living facility. You're afraid you might have to live out the rest of your life in a wheelchair. You're afraid of being a burden to others. Most of all, you're afraid of change."

She was staring at me. "That's true," she replied, slowly.

"And you're covering up all that terror—which is too big for you to address right now—with anger.

Anger at your daughter, your doctor, your injured back that has supported you uncomplainingly all these years, and your children. You're mad as hell at them all."

She nodded more vigorously. "I *am* furious."

"You're furious at your daughter for daring to advise you where or how to live. You're furious at your doctor for scaring you with the 'what-ifs' if you don't have surgery soon. You're probably even furious at your husband for getting so sick and dying on you."

This made her burst into laughter and sit up straighter.

"Already your back feels better, doesn't it?"

She looked thoughtful. "Maybe."

I felt she needed to wait before making any decision as drastic as surgery. There was no urgency—just pain. "Keeping still" was both the end and the beginning of all movement. If she could become still, and feel her fear and rage, it might begin to flow through her in unobstructed movement.[39]

I'd already watched the process begin.

How to Meditate

> *"Meditation is the journey from sound to silence,*
> *from movement to stillness, from a limited identity*
> *to unlimited space."* —Sri Ravi Shankar

When the Dalai Lama was asked what he would do if he were told he had only fifteen minutes left to live, he replied: "I would meditate."

I would too.

Many people have told me that the practice of meditation is too hard for them. The effort it takes to—as they see it—stop thinking is more than they can handle, and the more effort they put into meditating, the greater their frustration grows.

The practice of meditation is, in my experience, essential to experiencing stillness but not necessarily in the way people usually assume. Meditation is the mental equivalent to keeping our bodies fit, strong, and supple throughout our lives. Just as we need to move, to walk, to keep our physical body active and flexible, we need to keep our mental body strong and flexible as well. Physical activity takes a certain amount of conscious effort, whether it's going to the gym, doing yoga in the living room, or chopping wood in the backyard.

So does mental activity. We need to make a

conscious effort to keep our mental body supple and strong. We need to be in charge of it, not let it be in charge of us.

Meditation helps us achieve that, because through the practice of allowing our thoughts to move through us and not attach to them, we practice subtle but extraordinary control over our mental process.

The significant studies on the positive effects of mindfulness and meditation support the efficacy of stillness in quieting mental chatter so that we can experience the fullest expression of ourselves.[40]

When someone tells me they need more exercise but they hate going to the gym, my response is not that they should sit on the couch all day. I suggest alternatives. We find a way of incorporating physical activity into their lives so that they can enjoy it.

Similarly, there are many ways to meditate or at least to achieve mental stillness. We each need to find our own way. Sometimes a guided visualization is the solution, because it may be easier to focus on someone's voice rather than on your own mental chatter. Sometimes it may be helpful to concentrate on an image or listen to drumming or music.

It's not about learning not to think but to loosen your grip on your thoughts. Let them pass through your mind naturally and don't take them too seriously. Nonattachment sets you free.

The process of learning how to meditate has less to do with concerted effort and more to do with doing the best you can. Relaxing into a habit is the best way—habit takes the place of discipline, or of forcing ourselves mentally to do something we don't want to do. "Try hard, but don't try too hard," the Zen master Suzuki taught his students. "In zazen leave your front door and your back door open. Let thoughts come and go. Just don't serve them tea."[41]

Meditation can be focusing on a mantra or your breath, practicing mindfulness, walking, dancing, yoga, listening to music or a visualization, emptying your mind, or sinking into quiet stillness.

Thich Nhat Hanh recommends walking slowly and with awareness: "It can take a lifetime of practice to walk without letting our thoughts take us out of the present moment. ... Awakening to beauty has the capacity to shift one's whole perspective on life. ... Finding the silence within us makes space for true happiness."[42]

I believe that mindfulness is essential for mental calm and freedom, just as daily exercise is essential for good health. Don't underestimate it.

If you can move at all, then you can stretch and stay strong and limber.

If you can think, you can practice mindfulness.

Regular practice will stop the weak mental flabbiness that occurs when we allow our mental body to take over our reality, our stillness.

In my grandmother's—Ethel Cook Eliot's—iconic children's book, *The House Above the Trees*, Tree Mother has to go away for a while and she leaves the young Hepatica in charge of the forest. "But I am just a little girl," says Hepatica, who feels overwhelmed by the enormous responsibility being placed on her shoulders.

Tree Mother gives her only this advice: "When you need assistance, *let the forest think through you.*"

I have often used this advice for myself. Even when living in the heart of the city, I've been able to tune out all the noises to get to the heart of the stillness of the forest within me, "*within* the within of the forest," as Hepatica calls it. When that happens, I am filled with a profound quiet that allows me to know intuitively what needs to be done or said or heard.

You, too, can let the forest think through you. Allow the surface noise of your thoughts to drift away and the resonance of stillness in your mental body to remain. This is how to tap into intuition too. And how to understand the language of birds or other creatures: you let what you are thinking drift though you and away and you are left with *the bird thinking through you*. The more you practice this, the more you will feel in harmony with your surroundings, the people in your life, and yourself.

Find your own way of meditating. Running can be a meditation or walking in nature or focusing on your breath. If you want to begin with classic meditative technique and you haven't meditated before, here's a beginner's basic:

Find a place where you know you won't be interrupted. Sit comfortably. Close your eyes. For five or so minutes, focus on your breath. Breathe rhythmically and slowly. You'll hear your breath going in and out, and you might get twitchy and bored and begin to think of something else. Gently focus your mind back on your breath.

When images or feelings come to you, imagine they are rafts on a gentle river: just let them pass by. Focus on your slow breathing again.

After five minutes, quietly let go of your concentration and open your eyes.

That's it.

Over the course of the next few weeks, you may want to increase your meditating time to ten or fifteen minutes. Eventually you'll find the time that works best for you. Transcendental Meditation recommends a minimum of twenty minutes twice a day. Zen monks sit in meditation for six hours or more. Make your meditation practice your own.

If you already know how to meditate, but only do it on occasion, try to do it as a regular practice for a week and observe any changes.

If you're a seasoned meditator, then try a different kind of meditation for a week or two, to stretch and flex your meditation muscles. There are so many varieties to choose from: focusing on a mantra, walking, dancing, whirling.

Choose the one that works for you.

Breath of Life

> *"The Breath of Life unites all—she contains us and
> she is in us, like a fish in the ocean—and life
> without her is preposterous."* —Charles Ridley

It may seem like a paradox that the regular, sustained, conscious *movement* that is the essential aspect of breathing can bring us to stillness. But so it is. Movement and stillness are as interwoven as strands that create a tapestry.

Focusing on your breathing can be one of the simplest and more efficacious mindful meditations there is, and this you can do while walking, standing in line, trying to go to sleep, or when you first wake up.

"Just come into stillness," advises psychologist, author, and meditation teacher Tara Brach. "Have your intention be to relax with the breath. That will begin to set in motion a habit that will start to train the mind."[43]

Mindful breathing helps us to focus, and in energetic healing work it is more than that. It enables healing stillness to occur.[44] This is because breathing connects us with our energetic being. From the moment we take our first breath, we are filled with a basic human longing for union with Source. Each breath we take reminds us of that union.[45]

No matter how still we become, we always breathe, whether consciously or unconsciously. Through conscious breathing, we become aware of our stillness. Psychologists Wright & Wright remind us that "as we approach the still center from which the breath originates, we reach the level that extends beyond the outward show of energy and we approach the realm of pure spirit existing within us at the heart of all motion."[46]

With every breath release a thought.

When we watch these thoughts pass through us in a detached, unconnected, impersonal way, we can release psychological blocks as well. And even when everything around us seems to be chaotic or shifting, we realize there always exists an underlying stillness.

Paradoxical Stillness

> *"Every experience is a paradox in that it means to
> be absolute, and yet is relative; in that it somehow
> always goes beyond itself and yet never escapes
> itself." –T. S. Eliot*

When I was young, my parents took my brother and me on a freighter trip around the world and we spent long hours on the bridge of the ship. Often seagulls would come to where I leaned against the deck rail. They would hover in the wind, close to the ship and to me.

They did not appear to be flying, although their wings were outstretched. They did not appear even to be soaring. Because of the dual motions of the boat and the wind, they seemed completely motionless as they gazed straight into my eyes.

This was the paradox that I had to wrap my head around, that the boat was moving, that I was moving through space on the boat, that the wind was moving, the bird was flying—and yet no one and nothing appeared to be moving. Everything—including the seagull—seemed absolutely still.

To try to explain a paradox scientifically is not an easy task, but paradoxical thinking is at the heart of becoming still enough in our thoughts for creativity, inventions, and well-being to occur.

Einstein recalls how he first conceived his theory of relativity, which he called "the happiest thought in my life": "For an observer in free fall from the roof of a house, there exists, during his fall, no gravitational field in his immediate vicinity. If the observer releases any objects, they will remain, relative to him, in a state of rest, or in a state of uniform motion."[47]

Einstein imagined himself experiencing the paradox of falling and being still at the same time, which then allowed him to posit his famous theory.

Asking about the nature of light poses a similar paradoxical challenge. Light can be analyzed as either a wave *or* a particle *at the same time*.[48] Light is both a noun and a verb. A particle is a noun, a being. A wave is a verb, a becoming. Thus light is both stillness and motion—not at varying times and space but *at the same time and in the same space*.

That's a hard concept to imagine, but that *is* the physical nature of light.[49]

Quantum physics has opened us to a new science, which has to do with potentials and possibilities rather than facts and proofs. Physicist Werner Heisenberg noted that while some aspect of a subatomic particle can be measured (like, for example, momentum), its position could not be measured at the same time. The picture, in a sense, would always be fuzzy. He wrote, "the atoms and elementary particles ... form a world of potentiality or possibilities rather than one of things or facts."[50]

How is it possible for light to be both a particle and a wave at the same time? Or a subatomic particle to be both moving and in one position at the same time? One is still, it is an object, a particle. The other is a verb, it is in motion. Both these properties exist, paradoxically, together. Both are of the same nature.

But all basic dualities, such as uniformity and variety, peace and conflict, eternity and temporality, coexist *at the same time*. They do not become eradicated when one seems to dominate. The author and philosopher Avi Sion says, "At no level of existence or knowledge are the levels above, below, or adjacent to be considered as eradicated; they all coexist. All this may seem somewhat paradoxical, but it is the only way to reconcile differences."[51]

Janusian, or paradoxical, thinking—named after the Roman god Janus—involves holding two opposing ideas or images in one's mind at the same time, and offers an experience of stillness, enlightenment, and breakthrough. It allows imaginative concepts, ideas, inventions, and creativity to flow through us.

This was demonstrated in a 1971 study by Albert Rothenberg at Harvard University that involved Nobel Prize laureates in physiology, chemistry, medicine, and physics, as well as Pulitzer Prize– winning writers and other artists. It revealed a surprising similarity in their creative process: most major scientific breakthroughs and artistic masterpieces occur through the process of formulating antithetical ideas and then trying to resolve them.[52]

Janus was the Roman god of gates and doors, bridges, openings and closings, beginnings and endings, past and future. Represented by an image of two heads, each looking in opposite directions, this unusual god was worshipped at seasonal markers, such as planting and harvesting; at beginnings, such as marriage and birth; and during historical epochs, such as the transition from primitive to civilized cultures. Janus's namesake, the month of January, describes the gift he had of being able to see into the future as well as into the past—a gift he was given by the god Saturn. At midnight, on the last day of the year, he looks back at the old year, and at the same moment he looks forward into the new.

The breakthrough, or aha moment, that Janusian

thinking can engender can be achieved through stillness. When we have the paradoxical experience of being and becoming, our minds empty for a moment and a connection to our essential nature can occur. In a lecture on *Kabbalah and the Art of Being,* Shimon Shokek, "For every human being is a living organism, existing simultaneously in both change and stillness. This 'I' is not what the human being does but what the human being is, and therefore the activity of change and stillness together defines man's ontological nature."[53]

An example of experiencing being both the verb and the noun is in the paradox of thinking itself. We can think a thought, and as we are thinking it, we are also thinking about thinking the thought, which makes the object of the thought active rather than a noun of just 'thought.'

Aristotle tries to explain this in *Metaphysics*:

Thought thinks on itself because it shares the nature of the object of thought; for it becomes an object of thought in coming into contact with and thinking its objects, so that thought and object of thought are the same. For that which is capable of receiving the object of thought, i.e. the essence, is thought. But it is active when it possesses this object.[54]

Stillness takes us through the activity of thinking itself to becoming aware that we are thinking our thoughts.

Beyond thought and thinking is the equally remarkable paradox of presence and perceiving. Heidegger suggests that the Ancient Greek concept of *aletheia* (the translation means *truth*) is closer to meaning *presence*. "The quiet heart of the opening," he writes, "is the place of stillness from which alone there first is something like the possibility of the belonging together of Being and thinking, that is, presence and perceiving."[55]

We could even go so far as to say that in order to experience Source, we need to be aware of being aware that we are both the Source and the perceiver of Source. This is done, according to Heidegger, in the 'unconcealment' that occurs in stillness. He calls it a 'presence' and a 'presenting,' which can occur, paradoxically, at the same time. As Christopher Long reminds us: "Despite its being a site of quiet stillness, Heidegger nevertheless tellingly attempts to give voice to this opening that grants presence by articulating it in terms of the *Es gibt*, which carries the meaning of both 'there is' and 'it gives'."[56]

Stillness, like light, is both an objective state and a verb ("being still"). When we experience true stillness, it grants presence, to use Heidegger's phrase. It is giving and allowing. It becomes present by being.

We can integrate stillness into our lives by trying to hold two opposing thoughts or, even more difficult, two feelings at the same time. The train is moving, but when you touch the window, it is still. You are still as well, but you are moving through space. Experiencing the paradox of stillness and movement can only occur because we live in a physical dimension of time and space. When we allow both to occur at the same time, then we begin to understand the nature of stillness.

Practice this: hold two opposing views, or thoughts, or feelings at the same time. It's an extraordinary technique that can open the door to beyond stillness.

Water—Stillness in the Emotional Body

"Water is the driving force of all nature." —
Leonardo da Vinci

Getting in the Flow

Our precious water, which makes up more than 70 percent of our physical bodies and covers almost 80 percent of our planet, is a basic molecule made up of two hydrogen atoms and one oxygen atom. These three atoms form a strong bond that can hold a water molecule together for billions of years, and a single drop of water contains billions of water molecules.

Water is wonderfully versatile and transformational. When water freezes, its molecules move farther apart, making ice less dense than water, which is why ice floats. Water vapor is always present in the air, even if we can't see it; or it shows up visibly as steam or clouds. Then the vapor may attach to small bits of dust in the air, forming raindrops in warm temperatures and snow or hail in freezing temperatures.

This continuous water cycle, where water evaporates, travels into the air and becomes part of a cloud, falls down to earth as precipitation, and then evaporates again, repeats in a never-ending cycle. Water keeps moving and changing from a solid to a liquid to a gas, over and over.

This ability to move through the various processes in a circular flow is how a healthy emotional state continually changes and renews. Our emotions must flow, because if they become stuck, or dammed, they can upset or destroy us.

Water can dissolve more substances than any other liquid, and so can our emotions. Our emotions influence everything around us.

How we feel *is* how we are.

The Moon

"What other body could pull an entire ocean from shore to shore? The moon is faithful to its nature and its power is never diminished." — Deng Ming-Dao

The moon rules our emotional body. It's not just the tides that are higher during a full moon — we feel our emotions more intensely as well. Statistically, there are more babies born during a full moon. More crimes are committed then as well, and more accidents occur.

Our emotions are ruled by the element of water, so the fact that our emotions are affected by the moon makes sense, since water makes up more than 80 percent of our blood, 70 percent of our brain, and 90 percent of our lungs.

As the moon tugs on our planet's oceans, it also tugs on our blood, our brains, and our lungs. Is it any wonder that we feel a bit loony around a full moon? And that by the time a new moon rolls around we feel ready for our energy to increase and new projects to flow? By becoming increasingly aware of the phases of the moon and tracking the flow of our feelings at the same time, we can feel more still in our emotional bodies.

Try it. Notice your feelings during a full moon—
they tend to be heightened and intense. Teachers
report their classrooms being noisier, children acting
out more. Full moons amplify emotions, and enhance
fertility, virility, and transformation.

A waning moon is a time of release, hibernation,
and fostering energy. New moons are a time of
beginnings, promises, opportunity, and resolutions.

The waxing moon may inspire strong feelings of
creativity, forcefulness, growth.

The more we become aware of the moon's waxing
and waning energies, the more we begin to notice
how our own waxing and waning energies are
aligned with hers.

Intuition

> *"That is what the intuition is for: it is the direct*
> *messenger of the soul." Clarissa Pinkola Estes*

Water relates to our emotional body, which is
where our intuition lives. Intuition tunes all human
beings into their inner wisdom. Intuition is as much a
part of being human as is logical thinking, but science
and materialistic thinking has underestimated its

significance and importance in helping us to know who we are and what we need in order to realize our fullest potential.

What happens to most of us is that we confuse our intuition with our feelings, feelings which have been influenced by our mental analytical thinking. We have a hard time telling the difference between the two.

How can we tell the difference between our intuitive knowing and our logical reason?[57]

Our education and careers tend to engage our intellect and logic.[58] From an early age we are taught not to trust our feelings, whether that is a hunger pang or strong desire *not* to share a beloved toy. The brain is a wonderful tool. But it needs to be in our control. Too often, it is given way too much power over our intuition. We allow it to tell us not only what to do or say, but how to feel about something.

How do we tell the two voices apart: mental, anxious chatter from wise intuitive knowing?

Your mental chatter, your mind, speaks to you in a voice that is anxious, discouraging, fearful, worried. It's nervous, overactive, judgmental, and fearful. It nags, and makes you feel guilty. It's like little pinpricks when it makes you anxious or panicky.

On the other hand, your intuitive voice is always

calm. It's loving, encouraging, supportive, clear, and firm. Even if the intuition doesn't seem 'positive'—like don't go that party tonight or so-and-so's in trouble—the voice comes to you with a calm, reassuring stillness.

As soon as you can start to parse out those two ways of receiving information—mental logic versus inner knowing—you'll start feeling happier. You'll be more in the flow of your existence.

Our intuition typically resides in the realm of the unconscious. Often this has been confused with emotions, but intuition rests in the true feelings, not in the confusing and relentless, thought-induced feelings like shame, worry, guilt, and frustration. Stillness helps us to differentiate between these two. Stillness helps us experience guidance from our well of intuition—our knowing that comes from inner wisdom rather than from intellect.

The way to distinguish between thought-induced feelings and intuitive wisdom is to remove the thought that is bringing up feelings of shame, worry, or guilt. Without the thought, is the feeling still there or do you feel better and freer? Author and speaker Byron Katie encourages us to ask ourselves, "Who am I when I let go of a thought or a story I've made up about myself?"[59] When we let go of the story, what remains? An inner knowing—your intuitive, wise inner self.

Grow still and listen to the two voices vying for your attention. Don't try to stop your thinking, let your thoughts and feelings flow through you like a cool, sweet waterfall splashing into a secret pool in the middle of the forest. Refresh and cleanse yourself so that eventually only stillness is left.

Now what does your calm, quiet voice say? That's the one to listen to and trust.

Wu Wei

> *"How do I become still? By flowing with the stream."* —Lao Tzu

It might seem strange that finding our stillness happens through movement. But the element of water shows us how that is so.

"Stillness is Love. Movement is Life. To be still and still moving, this is everything," wrote Lao Tzu, creator of the *Tao Te Ching*, and this paradox is at the heart of healing our emotional bodies through stillness.

We tend to see much of our lives caught up in old

psychological debris. But these feeling states are like rocks, waterfalls, and rapids: they are part of the flow of life.

Move through them rather than getting stuck in them.

Again, it's all about surrendering to the flow of life instead of wishing it were different. Our intuition sees the flow clearly. It becomes a transcendent experience, a Tao of Stillness.[60]

We can learn to do this through practicing *wu wei*. The traditional translation is "nonaction" or "no action" but it's not entirely accurate, since in practicing wu wei, we *do* act. Wu wei means something more like "act naturally," or "effortless action." There's no need to live in any way other than in the flow of our reality.

When we follow the art of wu wei, we let nature take its course. We allow a river to flow toward the sea unimpeded instead of erecting a dam, which interferes with its natural flow.

We allow ourselves to move through barriers, debris, and stones rather than getting stuck and stagnant. We let life happen, and engage in it with curiosity and interest rather than force or control.[61]

I used this energy of water in trying to help a woman who was stressed and unhappy. She told me she was either exploding in rage at people around her or suffering from panic attacks, even though she was taking medication for anxiety.

We spent some time in stillness. I felt that everything seemed harmonious, healthy, and happy in her life. The tarot cards we turned over were ones like the Ten of Pentacles and Six of Cups—cards that reveal solid accomplishment and success as well as generosity of heart.

What could be wrong? What was damming up her free-flowing, generous, warm heart so that she was feeling blocked and angry?

"You're at a wonderful point in your life," I stated. "I don't see any challenges you're being asked to face."

"Then why do I feel so bad?"

"I don't think you do."

There was a pause, then, completely out of the blue, she mentioned that her daughter was getting married in a year. As she told me that, her demeanor changed. Her shoulders hunched, her brow furrowed, and her eyes saddened.

When she didn't say anything else, I prompted her. "And why is that stressful? Does it make you unhappy? Are you concerned about her fiancé?"

"No, he's wonderful. It's planning the wedding

that's terrible. My daughter and I fight about everything. We only have a year before it happens and we can hardly be in the same room without arguing. She just keeps on making terrible choices."

"Give me an example."

"The flowers. She wants red roses. But, of course, at a wedding you should have white roses. She just doesn't get it. That's just one thing. She won't wear my wedding dress because she says it's too frilly, and the one she's chosen looks ridiculous. It's practically see-through. My husband refuses to pay for it, so now they're fighting too."

"Tell me why her choices matter so much to you," I said. "It's her wedding."

"Well, we're paying for it—and it's not cheap!" she replied, sharply.

"Okay. I understand. But which do you want more—to have a wonderful year preparing your daughter's wedding or a year of stress and unhappiness?"

"Well, of course I want a wonderful year with her. I hate feeling like this!"

"Then choose to have a wonderful year. That's the river you're in right now. That's your current of life. You need to flow with it."

"You mean let her do whatever she wants?"

"Yes."

She shook her head firmly, pursed her mouth, and said, "I can't do that. Do you know what our friends would say to some of the choices she's making?"

"Do you want to feel angry because of what your friends might say or happy because your daughter is happy? You're entirely free to choose."

She looked up eventually. "Isn't it my job to set her straight though?"

"What does that mean 'set her straight'?" I asked. "Why does a friend of yours have more clarity about how your daughter would like her wedding to be than your daughter? Try untangling yourself from other peoples' expectations and your own preconceptions. What if there were absolutely no 'shoulds', no 'right-and-wrong' in the wedding world. Imagine that."

"That's hard."

"Try." I paused. "What if you allowed your daughter's happiness and desires to be your current of life and you floated along with her. Why not choose that instead of all these rocks and log-jams of 'shoulds'. Listen to her. Support her."

"She'd probably have a heart attack if I did that." She shook her head.

"I don't think so," I said.

"I know my husband would."

"They'll both be thrilled. And I see for you the most wonderful year of your life."

She smiled cautiously. "So that's my future?"

"If you choose it. Why argue about the color of the roses? Let her decide, flow with that, and you'll be so happy. You both will."

"I have to say, she's going to be surprised at this change."

"Great. I think your husband will too. You'll find he falls in love with the dress she's chosen."

"I don't know about that, but I'll try to persuade him to at least pay for it."

"That's a good beginning."

In the heart of stillness, she was able to give herself permission to let her daughter make decisions—without judgment. She realized that this could be the most stressful year of her life—or the happiest. She was free to choose how she would live it.

She could struggle against the current and worry about drowning or she could float along—no matter how hectic—in the flow of her daughter's happiness.

Dadirri and Listening

> *To know me*
> *is to breathe with me*
> *To breathe with me*
> *is to listen deeply*
> *To listen deeply*
> *is to connect*
> —*Miriam-Rose Ungunmerr*

The ancient aboriginal spiritual practice of *dadirri* exemplifies the use of stillness and listening for healing. Dadirri is an inner listening—being in quiet awareness of whatever it is that is going on.

When the mystic and counselor Miriam-Rose Ungunmerr speaks of dadirri, she is describing a form of contemplative listening that is akin to a personal spiritual practice. This type of listening in stillness is widely known throughout Australia and is an active practice used in healing.

> When I experience dadirri, I am made whole again. I can sit on the riverbank or walk through the trees; even if someone close to me has passed away, I can find my peace in this silent awareness. There is no need of words. A big part of dadirri is listening.[62]

As Jonathan Davis describes in his article called 'An Indigenous Approach to Healing Trauma,' being still and listening is used to heal trauma in many aboriginal cultures:

"In a culture where everyone is so well-practiced at listening that it becomes a spiritual art, it makes sense that when trauma occurred the people would come together and deeply listen to each other. ... The essence of dadirri ... is the creation of a space of deep contemplative, heart-based listening where stories of trauma and pain can be shared and witnessed with loving acceptance."63

Often, healing trauma comes from emotionally completing an experience that may have been physically completed long ago. Most of us have had experiences when we disassociated physically from our bodies due to either physical or emotional trauma, and, as transpersonal psychologist and psychiatrist Stanislav Grof describes it, we "check out."

For healing to occur we need to feel the trauma and release it, not suppress or disassociate from it. If we don't, it shows up in various manifestations all through our lives.64 We inadvertently trap the part of it we cannot handle, and store it away for later.

"Dadirri is a practice that allows us to open up this trapped pain and trauma in a sacred and held space and with the support of those around us, we can finally feel it in order for it to be released," states Davis.65

The practice of stillness can access and activate

this experience of emotionally feeling something even long forgotten, and letting it flow through and out. Feelings, too, are energy. It's when they are blocked that they become painful—when they are allowed to be felt and then released, the flow of energy continues in harmony with our nature.

Huna Insights

According to Hawaiian mysticism, our higher self can be reached only through our intuition. Hawaiian spirituality is based on a complex, tenfold view of the human being: our thinking, feeling, and physical natures, each of which is divided into three parts. The tenth being is the integration of all the others.

Like many modern-day psychologists, ancient Hawaiians believed that human beings have three 'minds': the rational mind, the subconscious/ unconscious mind, and spirit or higher-self mind. Our task in life is to integrate them, so each can nurture and care for each other. The first mind, the *uhane*, is the rational and egoic mind. The *unihipili* is the intuitive but also unconscious part, which author Max Freedom Long describes in the following way:

"A spirit which can grieve but may not be able to talk; something that covers up something else and hides it, or is itself hidden as by a cover or veil; a spirit which accompanies another, is joined to it, is sticky, and sticks or adheres to it. ... It desires things most earnestly. It is stubborn and unwilling, disposed to refuse to do as told."[66]

In other words, our unconscious emotions that constitute the watery element.

The Huna understanding of our human experience describes our conscious 'self' as being unable to talk to the higher self *except through the unihipili or intuitive, unconscious self.* It is through connecting with our emotional body that we move beyond our conscious thinking to an inner 'knowing.'[67]

Becoming still is a way to do this, or being in a state of what the Hawaiians call *nalu*. As well as referring to the waves or surf of the *moana*, or the ocean, *nalu* is also a verb that describes, for example, the condition of the waves. For us, it can mean taking on a form of mindfulness, or stillness, during which a shift of thinking can occur.

Kahuna shaman Stewart Blackburn generously entered into a correspondence with me at a time when I was wrestling with certain aspects of understanding stillness. Nalu, he told me, is a form of meditation/ contemplation where one holds a focus on something until a clear shift occurs within, usually a sense of release and pleasure. "Stillness is a necessary nutrient that allows one to process everything else. It's kind of like the bacteria in the gut; if the bacteria aren't there, even the healthiest of foods won't get incorporated."[68]

Nalu is also used to describe the amniotic fluid that surrounds and protects an unborn child. The word carries with it a quality of stillness. To nalu is to meditate, ponder, contemplate. "It's the antithesis of the idea of waves itself, water free of waves, so calm and still that we can contemplate what is below … or a mind free of the waves of thought and mental disturbance."[69]

Unconditional Love

Sara was a thin, no-nonsense female, with thick glasses, a sharp nose and eyes, and folded arms. Her outward appearance seemed to be one of self-sufficiency, aloofness, and vitality. Although she was born and raised in Western Europe, she emigrated to the United States in her late teens and had lived here ever since.

Nothing about her gave me the impression that she was someone who would normally seek out a metaphysical practitioner—she seemed pragmatic, and dismissive about almost everything we talked about before the session started: the lovely fall weather, a glass of water, or the town to which she recently moved.

I asked her why she wanted to see me, and she replied curtly: ""My parents both died when they were seventy-five years old. My seventy-fourth birthday is next week, so I know I only have a year left. And I do not know what to do with it."

"Are you in good health?"

"Yes, but so were my parents. I am not afraid of death. I just want to make sure I am doing what I need to do in this last year."

"Are you married? Do you have children?"

"No—neither."

I felt the need to help her soften, to make her feel safe so she could open up—all before we could address her question about how she should spend what she was convinced would be the last year of her life. She was way too closed for any good to come from this session. So I had her lie down on the couch, covered her with a soft blanket, and invited her to close her eyes. Through music and a visualization, I guided her into a meditative stillness.

It took longer than it usually did because I sensed she was tired...of life itself.

The only way to get through to her, I knew, was through her feelings. But they were so jangled up by her thoughts of loss and loneliness that they seemed to have disappeared underground. What was left of them appeared barren, dry, dusty, hard, withered, exhausted. How could we get moisture, succulence, refreshing water back into her emotional body?

I continued with the meditation, sinking her imagination into the earth, through underground streams, and sand, shells, riverbeds, trying to imbue her with the moisture of our beautiful planet and her own body.

After a time I sensed a gentle ease around her heart. I asked what was bubbling up for her.

She replied, dispassionately, keeping her eyes closed: "When I was seven, my uncle molested me. I was sitting on his knee, and my father—his brother—came in. My uncle blamed me and my father believed him. I was beaten and shamed, and neither of my parents spoke to me again. They brought our priest over, and I remember him saying, right there in front of me, 'well, at least you have another child.' That was my brother. He became everything to my parents. It was like I no longer existed."

Sara continued telling her tale in a low, neutral tone: How she hated her brother—how her brother had used their parents' horror at the event for his own manipulative purposes while they were growing up. How she had worked for thirty years in a mental health clinic, and how she had hated every single day of it. She never married, never had children. She did not know where her brother was, and did not care to find out. She was now retired and had recently moved to a new town, but she claimed her neighbors all hated her.

"It is because I am a foreigner."

I had noticed her accent. She said her family had emigrated when she was a teenager. "My neighbors sometimes cross the street when they see me," she said. "They refuse to talk to me. No one is there if I need help."

Her voice did not sound bitter, but her indifference seemed worse to me. And now she believed she had just a year to live and she didn't know what to do with it. I knew there was not much to say to Sara in terms of decisions to be made or an action plan to put into place. There was a lifetime that needed to be healed—and I honestly did not know if I could help her.

My work, as I continued to strum my meditation bowl, and to speak words that were as "watery" as possible, was to fill her up with the magical, healing quality of water. Water flows through us, and yet always replenishes itself. Water finds its own level, its own way. It is the strongest element because it perseveres through softness.

I set myself the quiet, persistent, determined task of unsealing the fountain of the emotional life within her. We explored her distant past, as though seeking the source of a river.

"What do you love?" I asked.

"Nothing," she replied, curtly.

"Do you remember what you loved when you were five years old?"

"No."

I asked her about her hobbies—how did she fill her time? There had to be *something*.

We continued to explore our quiet watery stillness together.

"I like my garden and my trees," she said, at last. "And the mountain I see from my bedroom."

At long last I knew how to reach her emotional body.

"Do you talk to the flowers? The trees?"

"Yes," she said, as though from a long way away.

"Do you see fairies? Or elves?" My tone was natural but her eyes opened and she turned to me in astonishment. Then, just as quickly, she closed them again.

"Sometimes," she said.

"Scientists now believe that every bit of matter has a sort of consciousness. It makes sense to imagine elemental beings as the consciousness of flowers and rocks."

I like to bring science in because people tend to be reassured if a scientist is mentioned, but in reality, I experience elementals as real with or without scientific proof, as did my grandmother and mother. I see them as the spirit, or consciousness, that exists in every living thing. I also know that we all experience elemental beings daily, even if we don't take notice of them. They surround us in vibrating, shimmering existence, a parallel dimension, that some of us can see or at least sense, but most of us aren't able to see or hear because we are limited by the five main senses of our physical body.

I searched for a book on my bookshelves. "Here, you'll enjoy reading this. You can borrow it, if you'd like."

She sat up and I handed her a book by the mystical author and artist Marko Pogacnik. She opened the book at random, and in her sharp, hard-edged voice read a paragraph aloud:

"First, elementals can exist on two levels simultaneously. Their bodies, unlike human bodies, have no material substance. Instead, they take the form of an energy vortex that vibrates on a vital-energetic level. Secondly, they have a consciousness which exists more on the emotional level, not on the mental level as with human beings. Therefore, they cannot be reached through thinking processes, but only through a feeling connection."[70]

She closed the book, studied the back cover, then the front, and looked thoughtful.

"Hm," she said.

"It's interesting to imagine that our feelings are a language we can use to communicate with. Did you ever have a pet?"

She shook her head.

"Basically, we communicate with animals through feeling. We also communicate with nature spirits through feeling."

"How do you mean?"

"The elemental world is like a parallel universe to ours. We can enter by moving through to a different dimension of space and time as though through a consciousness tunnel. It's done through an emotional connection, not a logical one."

Yes, it's only when we free ourselves from our logical, limiting way of thinking that we can delve into other kinds of consciousness, whether that consciousness belongs to an animal, a bird, a plant, a crystal, or an alien.

For the rest of our session, we talked about elemental beings and how each one is connected to a particular element—thus the name. Sara did not know much about them, and seemed interested to learn. I described how fairies, elves, gnomes, dryads or wood nymphs, and crystal beings are connected with earth. Sprites, mermaids and mermen, and undines are associated with water. Sylphs and imps are air beings. Salamanders are associated with fire. All these creatures work and play together to keep us and our mother planet in harmony and balance.

Near the close of our discussion, I said: "You can understand each creature's nature by delving into the nature of its element. A dryad, or tree nymph, will have a tree-like spirit, rooted in the ground and swaying in a breeze. Water creatures tend toward travel and adventure. Fire spirits move quickly and exude sparkle and light—I sometimes wonder what kind of picture do they have of our world? What are earth creatures, like elves and goblins, like?"

"They seem interested in what I do," she said, after a moment.

"Yes, definitely." I know that, although shy, elementals love communication with humans. They will be great healers for Sara. "Also, they tend to mirror back to us how we are—so if you're kind and generous, they will be as well. They love playfulness, mischief, fun, laughter." All this was energy that Sara needed desperately.

"And they care about our environment," she added.

"Yes, ask how you can help them," I suggested. "And you can also ask a favor from them. In return, leave a gift to show your gratitude. Anything sparkly, sweet, or lovely."

Communicating with elemental beings would be the first step for Sara to find her way to a satisfying, replenishing well of stillness. She'd be able to connect with them through the language of feeling, not French or another language. Feelings are vibrations, and when we vibrate in concert with our feelings, we feel in harmony with ourselves.

Because Sara felt safe enough to voice and connect with her love for the magical world of nature and the spirit within nature, she felt more alive and hopeful when she left.

Sara and I continue to see each other on a regular basis. During our sessions, we rarely discuss her past. Instead, each time we meet, I take her more extensively into topics and experiences that she can get emotionally connected with: crystals, flower remedies, the effect of fragrance on our psyches.

Through opening her up to strange or unusual insights through these experiences, she is gradually able to release a lifetime of pain. It's not that she will forget it or forgive it, or that she will be suddenly happy. It's that she now realizes it's part of the movement of life. She doesn't have to get stuck in it. She needs to continue to flow her way toward the sea.

Letting Go

> *Hanging from a cliff, let go-*
> *And agree to accept the experience.*
> *After annihilation, come back to life-*
> *I cannot deceive you.*
> *--Yuan Wu*

There is a chapter in *The House Above the Trees* in which the main character, Hepatica, is invited to play with Cloud, who is a Wind Creature. He, of course, can fly, and moves swiftly. He takes her hand and begins to run and climb through the air.

At first she is thrilled, but then she remembers that she is just a young girl and a human and immediately feels herself falling behind and pulling on Cloud's hand.

He shouts at her, "Let go!"

Misunderstanding him, she releases his hand and, out of breath and ashamed, comes to a standstill. He whirls around and demands to know what she is doing.

"You told me to let go," she says, trying not to cry.

He laughs at her. "I didn't mean let go of my hand!" he says. "I meant let go of yourself... I can pull you along without any problem. You need to let go of thinking that I can't!"

This is what Lao-Tsu means when he says flow is stillness and stillness is flow. When you let go of fighting the current, or believing it's up to you, you can flow with the wind, the current, the growing earth. And when you're in the flow, you are at peace.

Imagine our soul as a landscape with a lake. Tobias Kaye, the creator of the original sound bowl, paints the picture of the lake as our etheric body, and the lake is held by land, which is our physical body. Over the lake, the air passes, lit by moon and stars. Stillness allows winds of the astral body to abate. In a short time, the surface of the lake becomes calm and mirrors the moon.

He goes on to say: "The image of the moon in the lake appears to us as beguilingly beautiful. The everyday self, our normal identity, can be seen in this way. When we are upset, we lose sight of who we are and act out of the distress rather than out of a clear image of who we know ourselves to be."[71]

In the stillness of the water element we become the sky itself—not its reflection in a lake nor the clouds scudding across it. Our imagining that there is anything outside of ourself and beyond ourself is an illusion. Look at it this way: what we see in a mirror is not the reality—*the viewer* is. The reflection in the lake is not the reality: the sky is. But so often we behave as though *we* are the reflection.

So then, when ripples occur in the lake from a fish or a stone thrown in it, we feel affected. Stillness allows us to know that each individual is like the sky—we can feel unmoved by a pebble being thrown into a lake. Because when the reflection stills, we see ourselves as we are.

The beautiful tarot card known as the Hanged Man is a representation of letting things be as they are. We hang on to things, people, thoughts, and experiences throughout our lives, and it is sometimes one of the scariest things in the world to let them go. The Hanged Man reminds us that surrendering to what exists, to trusting in the universe, is a great practice.

It's also one of the most difficult lessons for most human beings.

Imagine a 'rope' in your life that you're hanging on to. It can be a big rope—like an unhappy career or a difficult relationship. Or it can be small—like a guilty thought that keeps nagging at you. Imagine how tired your arms are, how exhausted you feel, how you long for someone to come and help you back up the rope to where you were. Feel your loneliness: there's only you there, hanging on to that rope, legs dangling over the abyss. Maybe even cry a bit.

Now, instead of trying to climb back up the rope, imagine letting go. You realize that to hang on to a rope when your arms are aching is silly. There's no danger—everything around is soft and slow and warm and lovely. You're tumbling gently through a safe, interesting, always surprising world that is your creation.

Close your eyes and allow the best experience imaginable to come to you—don't try to force it. You might find yourself with a new way of looking at something that you were previously stuck on. That's what the Hanged Man does: he sees the world with a new perspective.

Maybe you feel relief.

The poet Robert Frost wrote "Stopping by the Woods on Snowy Evening" after having stayed up one summer night writing a long—and forgettable— poem called "New Hampshire." Exhausted, he went outside and saw the sun rising, and was suddenly inspired to write a poem "about the snowy evening and the little horse as if I'd had a hallucination in just a few minutes without strain."[72]

There's an ancient Zen koan that goes something like this:

You are holding onto a single branch with your mouth as you hang over the edge of a cliff. Below you is an abyss—

you can't even see its bottom. Your hands and feet are tied together with rope. Someone comes along and asks you, "What is Zen?" What do you do?

Letting go may be one of the hardest practices we choose in life, but when we do let go, extraordinary things can happen.

Practice Thanking Your Water

When I was ten years old, crossing a Jordanian desert with my travel-writer parents, I experienced for the first time an overwhelming thirst. Water was rationed during the interminable drive, and our guide told me I'd have to wait. When we finally arrived at a hot, dusty oasis where I was told there was a well, I was thrilled by the prospect of drinking water. Instead, the guide teasingly squirted water at my face from a wineskin, only a few drops of which went into my mouth. Everyone laughed; I wanted to weep from frustration.

Ever since that time, I've felt a special gratitude toward water. Even though I know I was not in any real danger, to this day I can't bear being thirsty. It scares me. I feel fortunate to live in a mountainous region, where a good well provides me with fresh, mineral-rich, plentiful water whenever I want it.

Like many teenagers, my friends and I used to have animated conversations about how every drop of water we drank had at some time or other been Plato's pee, or Theresa of Avila's tears, or tea drunk by Buddha, since there's a finite amount of water on the planet and it remains constant over time.

Every living thing on earth needs water, which makes it one of the most precious commodities. It's more valuable than diamonds, gold, real estate, food … anything, in fact. Water, like air, is at the core of our existence. But unless you happen to be crossing a desert where water is scarce, you may not pay much attention to this magnificence.

For many years I have consciously thanked and loved my water before I drink it. The mystic and healer Rae Chandran reminded me that, by doing this, the consciousness of the water is penetrated by my gratitude and love, and all water is healed.[73] This reminds me of Masaru Emoto's extraordinary experiments,[74] in which water that was spoken to in kind words and voice, crystalized in harmonious, exquisite, symmetrical patterns. When water was spoken to harshly and critically, the crystals were erratic, jagged, irregular.

Try it—see if the water tastes different, feels different if you speak to it lovingly before you drink it. Close your eyes and trust your intuition. Every time you drink some water, you are connecting with the flow of our soul's truth.

Water rituals the world over include gratitude and blessing; sometimes the ritual is as simple as pouring a few drops from your cup into the earth or into a stream.

A water ritual like this one does make a difference: We are drinking a lake, a cloud, his swamp, your tear ... every drop has been through every cycle imaginable, and by consciously loving it, we purify, honor, and send it on its way in a more beloved state, thus affecting our intuitive selves *and* the world.

Fire—Stillness in the Spiritual Body

*"Stop all doing and be still. Let the fire of stillness
burn everything and reveal That which is
Openness." —Adyashanti*

The Fire of Stillness

In our human experience, the element of fire correlates to the spirit because fire is the only element that requires a 'Prime Mover,' to use Aristotle's term, in order to be lit and it also requires energy to exist.

The flame that brings us to life and the fuel that feeds us throughout our human existence is the fire of Spirit. Fire is the element of warmth, transmutation, and light—and it is in the 'light' of our own spirit that we discover the stillness of Source. Thus, enlightenment is its essential nature.

Fire represents passion and creativity, purification, and alchemy. Fire occurs through the chemical reaction between oxygen in the air and fuel, such as wood or oil, which creates combustion. Our lives unfold in a process of spiritual combustion.

Fire is the only element that is not self-sufficient; in other words, water does not need fuel to exist, and neither does air nor earth. But fire needs a starting material, which is completely different to that which it transforms into. A log of wood from a birch tree becomes ash. Candle wax melts and burns away. The 'fire triangle' consists of fuel being heated, then reacting with oxygen to release heat energy, which results in combustion: and the fire is lit.

In the spirit world, our spirit becomes 'lit' by being enlightened. The triangle is similar: Fuel (whether it is creative project, invention, prayer, a helping hand, or, as in this exploration, stillness) is heated by our spirit's energy and love. When it encounters thought (that is, when we become aware of what we have done, or felt, or realized, the 'fuel' of accumulated habits), enlightenment ensues.

In Hegelian terms, the triangle would be seen as thesis—antithesis—synthesis.

I am not equating enlightenment with some kind of revelation or suddenly seeing God or angels or knowing what life is all about: enlightenment can be no more than a moment's fiery connection with an insight, or creative breakthrough, or transformational experience. Like composing a song or even kissing someone and realizing how much you love them, experience correlates with the element of fire and the nature of spirit.

So now how does that address spirituality and our spiritual nature? The word "spiritual" is often confused with "religion," which in turn implies dualism (human versus spiritual). For the purposes of this work, however, the words *spiritual* and spirituality refer to the potential spirit, or the signature, of each human being. In other words, being human *is* being spiritual, and the spiritual qualities we value, such as kindness, compassion, and love, are innately human ones as well.

In transpersonal psychology, we assume that what can broadly be called spirituality is an important part of consciousness and identity.[75] I believe stillness can unveil life's deepest mysteries of the soul and spirit through spiritual development. This is because our spirit is so much a part of our transformational experience.

Think about transformation. How do we transform? How do we evolve more and more into our fullest potentiality?

Through experience, yes.

And through initiation.

Five Great Initiations

We connect fire with transformation. And we can connect transformation with initiation. In our society, we tend to equate 'initiation' with being inducted into an obscure secret society, but that's not what we're talking about here.

We're talking about 'initiating' something new.

We're talking about committing to an experience that takes us through a portal so that we emerge enlightened and wiser than we were.

The Eleusinian Mysteries are among the most well-known of initiations from Ancient Greece. Although the actual rites of the annual initiation remain secret, we know that they were agricultural in nature and that they were based on the myth of Persephone and her mother, Demeter. According to the myth, the young, innocent daughter Persephone was abducted by Hades and kept with him in his underworld. Rebelliously, she refused all food, but ultimately was tempted to eat six pomegranate seeds. Her mother mourned and sorrowed, and the earth above became dark and cold. Eventually, a compromise was reached, and Persephone was allowed to be with her mother for six months of the year and with her husband, Hades, for the other six.

The initiatory rites of the Eleusinian mystery supposedly had to do with the cycles of life: Persephone's descent into the underworld; her mother's searching; and Persephone's ascent and reunion with her mother. But it is the profound transformation from innocence to experience that is at the heart of the initiation.

I regard our life's journey — as human beings — as being a series of initiations, both personal and collective. But there are typically five opportunities for great initiations that almost all of us experience. Navigating these is the constant in our lives.

Here they are:

Birth, which includes being born, also refers to any new beginning, a move, a new job, birthing a creative project, and so on. In the tarot, this initiation is represented by the Fool card, the setting off on a new adventure, a new journey. Mythologist Joseph Campbell calls it the "hero's journey," which we set off upon over and over, throughout our lives.

Adolescence is akin to the transformation a caterpillar makes to chrysalis in order to become a butterfly. This is one of the most tender and difficult of all the initiations, and, in general, it's the most underrated in most modern cultures.

Romantic love is treated as though it is a fairy-tale, a spike in endorphins, or a lucky chance rather than the extraordinary experience of connecting with our Source through the Other.

Sickness, which is regarded as 'bad' rather than as the much-needed rest it can be—or a wake-up call to compassion, empathy, or healing attention being called toward other aspects of self-growth.

Death, the ultimate end, can be considered another birth, but one that requires preparation of a different sort.

We have no control over any of these passages that we experience in this life—except in the way we respond to them and grow into more of our individual potentiality from them. Except for the first initiation of being born, we either take for granted or try to avoid the rest: We tend to ignore, deride, or worry about the enormous and dramatic inward experience of adolescence in ourselves and in others, we avoid getting sick when we can, we typically become strangled and confused by love, and we dread death.

However, having gone through each of these initiations, we are transformed in ways that have a permanent effect. Like learning to read, and realizing it is impossible to go back to the time when you couldn't read, each initiation takes us through portals that are impossible to retreat from.

Whether these initiations are actual or symbolic (i.e., the initiation of 'birth' can symbolically be a new beginning or leaving behind a previous life, so that we can start something new), these major life transitions and transformations can be experienced more fully and vitally when we allow stillness to occur.

Initiation is the fuel for the fire of our spirit.

Initiation of Birth

> *"The Fool represents the soul's entry stage into terrestrial consciousness, following its descent from eternity... The innocent soul is naked, an unadorned spiritual essence viewed at the literal dawn of its journey through the stages of life."* — Ed Buryn

In the tarot, birth and new beginnings are symbolized by the iconic card known as the Holy Fool.

In many decks, the symbol of new birth is

represented by a young man who is not looking where he is going but at a passing butterfly as he is about to step off the edge of a cliff. The feeling we get is of blithe optimism and adventure. This is not an image of courage or thoughtfulness. When we plunge into something new, we do it without having a clue about what is in store for us.

But we are willing to explore. We are willing to find out.

The Fool is optimistic, naïve, trusting, carries with him everything he needs, has a companion, and sets off the edge of the cliff into a cloud of unknowing, trusting that he'll fly, instead of fall, into his next adventure. If he does fall, he trusts that he'll be able to pick himself up and go on.

This is the essential nature of being human—we are optimists. We are all basically 'fools,' or in Joseph Campbell's terminology, 'heroes.' We are on a hero's journey through life, facing the trials and tribulations, challenges and joys, twists and turns with enormous courage and love.

We take our first steps with awe; we start school with excitement even if we're anxious; we fall in love—usually more than once, even if we've been hurt. With what amazing stamina and grace do we venture forth through this great story of our lives! It continues to astound me to witness the immensity of sacrifice, kindness, and energetic goodness that most people pour into their lives and into the lives of others.

Becoming still in these moments of 'birth' means that we can allow the serenity, clarity, and confidence to be able to let the next adventure open up for us.

Childbirth

I like to think of birth as something the child being born is doing, rather than the parent. The mother is the land where the ship is coming to dock. If a birth is long and complicated, the spirit of the child may be cautious and needs extra time and encouragement. When a baby bursts enthusiastically onto the scene in a surprisingly short time, notice how that's their energy throughout their lives.

Instead of concentrating so hard on the mother's, her partner's, and the medical professionals' concepts around the birthing process, how about focusing on the soul of the child that is being born?

Here is a soul that is 'dying' to the light-filled, high vibrational atmosphere of the spiritual world to be incarnated into a physical body that is dense and painful. What a journey! Imagine loved ones, angels, and elementals gathering around to tell the baby, "goodbye and good luck," while on this side of the veil we are anticipating the arrival of this new life.

How might stillness help in pregnancy and the birthing process?

If we could become still during childbirth, and allow the soul to 'die' from the spiritual world (which for some souls might be difficult), and then welcome the baby into this incarnation by surrounding them with the stillness and peace that reminds them of whence they came, they will thrive, and the parents will thrive as well.

This example refers to our 'first' birth—the time and place that becomes the point of origination on this plane. But the initiation we call "birth" also refers to all new beginnings.

Let's be still in the center of chaos and the unknown.

Creative Beginnings

Almost all creative and inventive endeavors emerge from a place of stillness. Benjamin Hoff, author of the Tao of Pooh, calls it a place of 'Nothing':

> Let's say you get an idea—or, as Pooh would more accurately say, *it* gets *you*. Where did it come from? From this something, which came from that

something? If you are able to trace it all the way back to its source, you will discover that it came from Nothing. And, chances are, the greater the idea, the more directly it came from there. 'A stroke of genius! Completely unheard of! A revolutionary new approach!' Practically everyone has gotten some sort of an idea like that sometime, most likely after a sound sleep when everything was so clear and filled with Nothing that an Idea suddenly appeared in it.[76]

The poet John Keats calls it *negative capability*, "that is, when a man is capable of being in uncertainties, mysteries, doubts, without any irritable reaching after fact and reason."[77]

Mystics, poets, and philosophers have used the term negative capability to note a quality of 'nothing' or 'stillness' wherein an individual can experience ideas, inventions, creative sparks, and strokes of genius that go well beyond what they thought they were capable of. The philosopher Jean Klein says, "The threshold of truth is the absence of calculation, the not knowing state. All that appears in you refers to this thoughtless ground, your silence. Every object appears and dies in this stillness."[78]

All true artists, whether they know it or not, create from a place of no-mind, from inner stillness, as Eckhart Tolle says. It is in that stillness, we become free: we can think, feel, and create whatever we want.

In that stillness, flashes of inspiration, profound

insight, sublime poetry, or the answer to a conundrum show up, seemingly by magic.

If we could allow stillness to imbue us during moments of new beginnings, choices, decisions, experiences, we'll find the clarity to embrace the change, creativity, and new beginnings that are constant throughout our lives.

Initiation of Adolescence

> *Your Thundering Years mark your journey into*
> *adulthood—into your independence—a time of*
> *longing, of lost and found, of power, and of*
> *crossroads. Sacred wisdom refers to it as a "heroic*
> *journey" full of pitfalls and magic."*—Julie Tallard
> Johnson

Adolescence is the time when we are in a chrysalis. We are processing that great shift from caterpillar to butterfly. It is far more dramatic than the change from baby to toddler, because the development occurs not just on physical level but on a deeply personal and emotional one.

This is the time when our emotional body is becoming embodied within our growing selves. That means that our emotions need to have the most protection, nourishment, tenderness, and respect, even more than our physical bodies or academic studies. In our typical impatient culture, grown-ups way too often grow impatient with the intensity of the feelings of their children as they emerge in adolescence. They tend to belittle, or rage back, or punish.

There's another way. It has to do with stillness. It

has to do with allowing a teenager's emotional rollercoaster and development of their heart's desire and soul's longing to be left alone to work through their struggle with independence—while honoring them, keeping them safe, to listen to them when they need to be heard, and to be present without interfering with their need for privacy.

Adolescents tend toward questioning, asking, seeking—this is their nature. Our task as adults is to nonjudgmentally encourage their questions (not always to answer them but to show them ways of finding out for themselves). It's to enrich their imaginative powers and to develop their compassion for others. Their healthy emotional life develops in them through relationships, including friendships with extended family, multiple teachers, and mentors. Here is what Julie Tallard Johnson says about the importance of adolescence, which she calls the "Thundering Years":

Ultimately, the Thundering Years are a time of choices. Some find a passage in a book. Or, a stranger says something that sticks with us; a story touches our soul and opens a new door; an oracle guides us on the right path; or we have a dream that won't let go. Through chance and synchronicities we find our way to what we need.[79]

Their social lives are far more important than their academic accomplishments, and far too under-rated.

The most important thing we can do as grown-ups is to inspire a real interest in the world around our teenagers, whether it's artistic, humanitarian, research-based, or inventive. When they're thrown back into themselves and become self-centered, they are drawn toward power, callousness, or hopelessness.

Rudolf Steiner recommends that teenagers

> "must be led to look out into the world around them and into all its laws, its course, causes, and effects, into human intentions and goals, not only into human beings, but into everything even into a piece of music, for instance. All this must be brought to them in such a way that it can be sounded over and over within them so that questions about nature, about the cosmos, and the entire world, about the human soul, questions of history, and riddles arise in their youthful souls."[80]

The most beneficial act that an adult can provide a teen during this initiation is to encourage and grow their capacity for idealism and empower them to create ideal situations in the world. One way to do this is to introduce them to the history of radical leaders and wise healers, people who strive to change the world for the better. Having greatness as guides—writers, musicians, leaders, inventors— reminds teens that there is a world out there that they can master and become a part of. And it affirms that if they are strong—from the inside out—they can embrace a path toward that mastery.

Pain only becomes greater the more we think about it, as Steiner says, and when teens become too engrossed in their pain and suffering (which is very real) without being given tools that will take them outside themselves, the subjectiveness of their experience can turn to alarming hopelessness and depression.

Adolescence is a time to come into contact with ideals, heroes and heroines, great deeds and accomplishments, people who have made a difference, admirable causes, activism, and love.

Teens thrive in nature

Research continues to evolve on the effect of nature on teens. For instance, the increasingly popular Forest Schools are expanding into the high school years. Forest Schools were originally started in Denmark as a type of early childhood education that embraces the outdoors, sometimes with no actual building but only the woods and fields and other outdoor environments as the school.[81] In these early childhood programs, children thrive in ways that being forced to sit still in a sterile environment does not allow.[82]

Increasingly, psychologists and scientists are

researching and demonstrating the benefits of nature on teenagers. Some examples are Native American retreats, Waldorf farm and gardening programs, and orienteering and wilderness training.

Being in nature is tremendously helpful during the topsy-turvy time of adolescence. Teens understand better than grown-ups the paradox of being still while in motion: watch them discover an unfamiliar mushroom or hear the song of a rare bird. They often, naturally, become still and observe. Every sense becomes heightened and alert. The experience takes them out of the intensity of their inward feelings and helps them become more objective and caring about the world around them.

As Eckhart Tolle reminds us, listening to the silence is one of the easiest and most direct ways of becoming present and still. "Even if there is noise, there is always some silence underneath and in between the sounds. Listening to the silence immediately creates stillness inside you."[83]

Daydreaming into Stillness

One of the qualities parents and teachers notice in teenagers is their tendency toward daydreaming. They drift off or tune out as the grown-ups are asking them to wash the dishes, do their homework, or go to bed. *Remember to turn off the light ... don't forget to call me ...* and they don't remember and they do forget, mainly because they are daydreaming through the experience of this incarnating time into their full adult selves.

Yet we neglect to allow teenagers enough time to daydream. There's always something that has to be done, or learned, or memorized, and a teen's intense need for zoning out is then, generally, experienced through screen time instead of daydreaming.

We don't value daydreaming in our culture. Mostly, it has a seriously negative connotation in our busy lives. Dr. Freud even called daydreaming "a neurosis" and many people still believe that.

But neuroscientists describe the brain as having two separate 'networks': an administrative network, which we use when we're busy accomplishing a task, and a default network, which is the one that we default to when we're taking a nap or watching TV. In other words, the default network 'switches off' when we need to focus. And when one network is 'lit up,' the other is not.

However, when we daydream, *both* networks are lit up at the same time. In other words, when our mind is at rest and allowed to wander, it is *more* active than when it is engaged in a task.

In an article in *Scientific American,* author Marcus
E. Raichle describes this research and how significant
'doing nothing' is:

> "A great deal of meaningful activity is occurring in the
> brain when a person is sitting back and doing nothing
> at all. It turns out that when your mind is at rest—
> when you are daydreaming quietly in a chair, say, [or]
> asleep in a bed or anesthetized for surgery—dispersed
> brain areas are chattering away to one another. And
> the energy consumed by this ever active messaging,
> known as the brain's default mode, is about 20 times
> that used by the brain when it responds consciously to
> an outside stimulus. Indeed, most things we do
> consciously, be it sitting down to eat dinner or making
> a speech, mark a departure from the baseline activity
> of the brain default mode."[84]

There are lots of theories as to why this may be so,
but nothing conclusive, except this: people who are
prone to daydreaming, and whose networks are
working simultaneously, score higher on creativity
tests and are more able to think innovatively and
originally. Research has also connected daydreaming
with healthy social adaptability and improved work
performance.

Being still and daydreaming is not the same as
reading a book or watching a movie, or meditating,
or focusing on a mantra for a prescribed set of
minutes. No, it's looking out the window and not
thinking much about what's there. It's taking a walk

with no pre-decided destination. It means allowing yourself to be what we often think of as "bored." It's letting go of all those heady shoulds and musts and have-tos, and instead letting mullings and musings come to you. It's opening yourself, finding a place that is so quiet you become one with the world. There's no effort involved in daydreaming, in letting your mind rest, just as there's no effort in the central activity of breathing.

When we encourage teenagers to daydream, we encourage the development of their creativity and confidence. Stress in teens can sometimes take decades to recover from. Something as simple as allowing more time for daydreaming can alleviate the long-term suffering that otherwise may ensue.

As a teenager, when I'd get home from school, my mother would make us a pot of tea and we would sit on the couch, mostly in silence. She knew I was not much of a chit-chatter, and the stress of being asked how my day was would probably drive me to my room. Instead, we would sit comfortably together in quiet, sipping our tea, and feeling connected in a different way than talking. We called these times our 'nonverbal conversations.'

I believe there is great value in nonverbal conversations for true, or soul, communication between human beings. Quaker meetings are a case in point—a gathering of people sitting in stillness and in silence together.

How can we bring that community stillness into our educational system? For example, when two children are involved in a bully versus victim relationship, one way of moving them through the divide is to have them work together on a project or do a chore together. But might having them both walk together in nature in silence, or sitting together in stillness have a profound, and perhaps more lasting, effect?

Try being in stillness with your teen, instead of feeling riddled with worry, resentment, or guilt about whatever it is you imagine is going on. Try allowing your teen to have time for stillness, let it be okay for them to be still and quiet.

And no matter how old you are, remember your own initiation of moving from chrysalis of childhood to the butterfly of adulthood. Does your own adolescence need tender attention and healing? You can revisit that time, and soothe your adolescent soul through visualization, kindness, trust, and reassurance from your current vantage point of the wise adult.

Initiation of Romantic Love

"No relationship can thrive without the sense of spaciousness that comes with stillness." –Eckhart Tolle

On average, I would estimate that at least three quarters of my clients come to me for guidance around their relationships in general, and the majority of these clients want help with questions of romantic love, whether that entails finding 'true' love, wondering about a life partner, marital issues, loneliness, betrayal, or grief when a partner leaves or dies.

Romantic love is the theme of most popular songs and shows up in most novels. It's on the minds of most people, generally. When we're in love, our lover is our focus. When we're not in love, we're wondering why not.

I believe that romantic love brings to consciousness an understanding of the great mystery of life itself.

Romantic love between two people may change over the years, and may emerge in various forms through the decades. But the yearning for it and the mystery surrounding it does not change. Some people believe teenagers are too young to fall in love or that it's laughable to see elderly people falling in love. But romance shows up unrestricted and unruly, rarely abiding by anyone's expectations. If it's not present in someone's life, it is still mysteriously yearned for.

This fact, it seems to me, shows that romantic love is a vital aspect of our human existence. It's more crucial to our humanity than romance movies or dating apps would have us believe. The cultural cynicism around romance dims its power and significance. The perseverance and exhaustion that people are willing to endure for the sake of romantic relationships is undermined by that cynicism.

I would like to disarm that cynicism and replace it with the grace of romantic love that shows up in myths like the one that tells of Eros and Psyche. Romantic love is a marriage of soul and heart, and in that union we find wholeness, not just on our life's path, but on our inner journey as well.

Here's a brief re-telling of the Psyche-Eros story: Psyche was a princess of such beauty that Aphrodite, famous for being the goddess of beauty, became jealous. She instructed her son, Eros, the god of love, to punish her. Eros was so stunned by Psyche's beauty, however, that accidently he pricked himself with one of his legendary arrows of love, and instead of punishing her, he rescued her from the terrifying rock in the middle of the ocean on which she had been imprisoned by Aphrodite. Psyche felt herself being lifted and carried to a magnificent palace.

Eros, being a god, could not reveal himself to her. However, every night, in the pitch dark, he came to her, a mysterious and loving being. Although she could not see him, she knew him to be tender and kind, so she submitted to his request that she never attempt to see his face.

Although Psyche was happy to be so well-cared for by her ardent, albeit invisible, lover, her jealous sisters persuaded her to try to see what he looked like. After all, he could be a monster! One night, while Eros slept, she lit a candle, tiptoed to the side of the bed where he lay, and there beheld a supremely beautiful youth. In her delight, she stumbled and pricked herself with one of his arrows, thus finally falling in love with the god whom she had hitherto only loved because he loved her.

Then a drop of melted wax from the candle woke him with a start. He reproached her bitterly for her faithlessness, and vanished.

It took a long time, and many arduous ordeals, for

the star-crossed lovers to finally reunite.

Psyche's name means *soul* in Ancient Greek and in our era it relates to our own personal psyches. I relate their story because I believe the coupling of the human soul — or psychology — with divine love is at the heart of all metaphysical healing, and that falling in love is an essential aspect of that experience.

There is an old Sufi story about the seeker who visited a great sage to ask for spiritual guidance. He begged the master to be allowed to remain and study with him. The sage asked him, "Have you ever been in love?"

At once the seeker scoffed at the idea that one as spiritually evolved as he would waste time allowing himself to fall in love. The master told him that until he had experienced romance, until he had actually fallen in love with someone, he could not apprentice with him.[85]

Why does the sage believe that falling in love is a prerequisite to *all* spiritual development? The monks and nuns of monasteries and convents through the ages *fall in love* with Christ and marry him. The ecstatic Sufis *fall in love* with the Beloved, the great Friend. Practitioners of bhakti yoga work toward a union with the divine or self through love and devotion. It teaches us 'love for love's sake.' The

Sanskrit word *bhakti* is rooted in the original word *bhaj*, meaning "to adore or worship God."

We may all agree that romantic love exists as a fact of life, but I'm going to posit the possibility that experiencing romantic love imposes an important duty upon us as well. The duty to love and to be loved in as beautiful and artistic a way as possible may be a significant initiation of a sort that is beyond biology, family, culture, or even emotion—it has to do with our evolution and development of human consciousness.

Why do we fall in love? It can't be solely for the purpose of procreation, since less-evolved species are much more concerned with procreation than are humans, and more successful at it. The more intelligent, the less procreation seems to be important. Romantic relationships are not necessarily conducive to having lots of children.

We can regard falling in love either as a fact of nature or as a divine gift, but in either case it's a natural process that seems to arise independently of us, and without our permission. If neglected, it vanishes. It's as though romantic love directs us to a higher end—evolutionary wisdom that opens us to the whys and wherefores of existence.

In the introduction to Vladimir Solovyov's book

The Meaning of Love, Owen Barfield compares romantic love to the human capacity for speech. He describes how language has developed over the millennia. We would still be muttering and grunting if we had not developed this faculty, and eventually used it to write beautifully as well as to speak artistically. Barfield believes that the development of language mirrors the development of human consciousness, and so does the development of romantic love.[86]

What would happen if we regarded romantic love as beautiful, wonderful, and initiatory, and as essential to the future of human development as the use and development of language was in the past? The task of love is in justifying through deed the feeling we experience of being 'in love.'[87]

The true significance of falling in love is not in the experience of romantic emotion, but in what is accomplished by means of that feeling, in the *act* of love.

Could it be possible that love is a crucial stage of human evolution, and romantic love is the actualization of that evolution? If that is so, then it behooves us to regard romantic love with respect, tenderness, and value. We need to relate to our lover with the eyes of acceptance and appreciation. By valuing the other person in a relationship, we learn to value ourselves. By treating someone we love in ways we long to be treated, we learn about reciprocity and how love can be nourished and pruned and fertilized and cared for and thus how it grows and continues to grow.

Adolescents who think that it's okay for romantic and sexual relationships to be casual or purposeless, need to be encouraged to elevate their profound experience of falling in love to a higher, more mystical level. And adults who long for romantic love and passion can learn to regard this longing not as a weakness, or selfishness, or hopeless passion, but as an evolutionary experience into becoming themselves.

So, what role does stillness play in this initiation of falling in love?

It has to do with developing the feminine archetype within each one of us that understands *receptivity*. The sometimes unbearable longing, passion, and frantic pursuit for human love needs to be shifted to *allowing* love to occur through stillness: allowing ourselves to love and to be loved—by another, by the self, and by our Source.

It is in stillness that we stop wishing that a partner or friend were different than they are, and instead allow them to be exactly as they are *now*. And it is accepting another human being exactly as they are, in stillness, that relationships can evolve, change, improve, or dissolve.

Eckhart Tolle reminds us that "stillness cannot and need not be created. Just be receptive to the stillness that is already there, but is usually obscured by mental noise. ... If spacious stillness is missing, the relationship will be dominated by the mind and can easily be taken over by problems and conflict. If Stillness is there, it can contain anything.[88]

Or as Beach Boy Brian Wilson sings so sweetly:

> Don't talk, put your head on my shoulder
> Come close, close your eyes and be still...[89]

A client came to me asking whether she would ever be married. I knew that she was asking about more than just a future spouse. Her real question had to do with a painful loneliness. What she wanted to know was, "How can I feel joyful and loving, in my life?"

My sense was that she had forgotten ways to love—not just a partner, but friends, her home, her work. During our session, I endeavored to show her ways to connect with people, with the natural world, and with herself in loving ways. I asked her to remember activities she used to love as a child and to describe some elements in other people who she loved, so we could find them in herself.

I felt that by guiding her to experience a connection with Source and love, she could relearn how to love herself and her life as it was now. Falling in love with herself was her key to creating romantic love with someone in her future.

When we realize that we are partners in the manifestation of our destiny, not passive recipients of a future-train that is bearing down on us, we can manifest romantic love in our lives. This manifestation is not through pursuit but through allowance. The gift of stillness empowers each one of us to activate our own fullest potential—in freedom and in love.

"The Love of my Life"

What do people mean when they say, "He's the love of my life" or "She's the love of my life"? Typically, they are referring to one of their earliest, passionate, most 'in' love experiences, not always the person they ended up marrying.

But *is* that the love of their life? Wouldn't the love of their 'life' be the person they married, had a family with, and aged with?

Here's an example: A client had been married to her husband for thirty-five years. They had experienced many ups and downs, including several frustrating years in marriage counseling. They'd had three children together, busy (albeit separate) careers, and a few years of retirement. Now, her husband was dying, with just a few months to live. Hospice was helping, but my client was carrying the brunt of the burden of care, including trying to manage their children's grief.

In our session, she declared almost guiltily: "What makes taking care of him particularly hard is that my husband was not the love of my life. It's been a very difficult marriage—many, many challenges. You see, I'd been in love with another man—*he* was the love of my life."

Over the course of the next few weeks, with gentle prodding, she began to alter her perspective, and to see that her husband actually *was* the love of her life. The relationship may not have been a fairytale, but it was better than that: It was real.

Real love, real romantic love, is not what we may imagine—it may be hard work, ups and downs, even separations and reunions.

As our weekly sessions continued, my client began to speak more tenderly about her husband,

and about herself, as well as their relationship. Through the stillness that occurs when death shows up, there was a shift in her consciousness. She saw how her husband, the man she'd lived with during all the tempestuous, exciting, boring, happy, sad decades, *was* the love of her life.

Her fantasy for a romance that had never existed dissolved like mist only once the real love of her life lay dying.

Transpersonal Romance

If you love life with all your heart and soul, with energy, ferocity, and protectiveness, with enthusiasm, passion, and commitment, you will find that you live a life that contains all that as well. Marriage, children, family are a by-product.

Transpersonal romance shows us that beyond everything else is the fascination, hunger, thirst, interest, pleasure, enthusiasm, curiosity, wonder, and enjoyment in life itself—not what it means, nor what will happen, nor what has happened, nor success or fame or anything, except the experience of loving life itself.

The more we understand 'why' the experience of romantic love is so important, the more we can create rituals and experiences to benefit from them and offer guideposts and cautions for the journey.

Of all the human experiences most fraught with tangled webs of psychological trauma from early relationships, past life issues to resolve, ancestral and spiritual DNA, and the vital need to fulfill one's own individual potential in this incarnation, romantic love is the initiation most archetypal and universally experienced, and at the same time the most personal. Birth is something we go through with openness and naivete—with innocence. Adolescence is almost an unconscious awakening, rather like learning to walk. Sickness is enmeshed in a personal journey of individuation and self-growth. Death is being born into the unknown and requires its own map and directions.

But romantic love shows up repeatedly, shyly, embarrassedly, tentatively, longingly, and even desperately. There are more songs written about romantic love than any other subject. If a book doesn't have some romantic attraction in it, even if peripheral, it's hard for most readers to get engaged. Films, Shakespeare plays, and ancient Greek dramas all center—for the most part—around romantic love.

As I said earlier, in my metaphysical practice it is rare that a client does not have romance at the heart of any question or request for guidance. They might couch it in questions about career or aging parents or whether they should move from hither to thither — but as we dig into the real issue it almost invariably has to do with romantic love.

Sometimes it's a despairing on-again-off-again romance that they can't let go of. Or it's a longing for passion, which in some people exists till the day they die. For others, it's a longing for companionship, which is a form of romance for some people. It even shows up in an adamant 'never again!' energy, that informs me of a challenge around romance.

Romantic love comes in all shapes and sizes, all colors, all fragrances, all shadows, and delights. It is not the Cinderella fantasy that many girls imagine romantic love to be, and nor is it a business merger that seeks to combine career, family, and personal self-care.

I believe that being in love and being beloved by the one we love is one of the most powerful and motivating forces that drives us as human beings. But over the course of centuries and cultural, political, and familial distortions, we have forgotten how significant and life-changing falling in love can be.

When we can experience romantic love out of a place of stillness, a remarkable thing happens: we realize how much love is inherently our nature. Too often, we think of love as one more "watery" emotion, akin to like or dislike. But love is distinctly different from opinion or anything even remotely negative.

Love is mystical and romantic love needs to be elevated to that level.

Love is our true nature, and therefore the experience of romantic love can be gleaned through stillness.

Walt Whitman describes his own mystical love affair with life this way: "I know that the hand of God is the promise of my own, And I know that the spirit of God is the brother of my own, And that all the men ever born are also my brothers and the women my sisters and lovers, And that a keystone of the creation is love."[90]

How can we understand, know, and feel love?

The answer can be found in stillness. Stillness allows love to exist. Stillness also allows us to love ourselves.

We've been programmed to think that selflessness and doing good deeds for others are vital for our well-being. We've been told that sticking with a lousy job, an abusive boss, or a bleak sacrifice is what life is about. Self-denial is part of our existence.

That's all true, to an extent. But it's not the complete story. What matters most in the world is *each one of us becoming our fullest potential*. That means we need to care first and foremost about our self. Everything we do and care and feel and think needs to be with each one of us at our center, no one else.

Like a sun with its galaxy of planets and stars, we need to be our own suns. We need to remain in the still center of our universe, without being sucked into other peoples' orbits—whether they are our children, lovers, or colleagues. By imagining ourselves as miniature suns, we see what it is like to be still and yet shine our energetic, warmth and light on the people and tasks in our life. In this way, our light shines on everything and everyone and they can flourish and grow and shine as well.

By loving ourselves, I'm not advocating selfishness or greed! It's the opposite, in fact. Greed is *not* loving yourself—greed and selfishness will make us sick, just as it makes the world sick. Loving ourselves means being as kind and loving toward ourselves as we would be toward someone we love dearly.

That's all very well and good, I hear you say, but how can we do it? Years of conditioning, and of people telling us the opposite (*Don't be vain! Don't be selfish!*), and measuring our value in terms of wealth, attractiveness, or success, make it feel impossible. So what is the process? How can we practice this?

By turning it around. How often do we exclaim: "I love that poem!" Or, "What a great song—I love it!" When we turn the experience around, something shifts in us. Poems, songs, paintings, a sunset, a bird, a candle—they all want to love us. Let them.

Letting ourselves be loved is how we can touch, light up, and activate the loving stillness that is our core.

Then it is that stillness becomes synonymous with love. When we see the higher self of any being who comes into our orbit, we can't help but love.[91]

When we look into the human soul with the eyes of divine love, we have encountered the true power and magic of metaphysical healing. We need love to help, guide, heal, and evolve.

As St. John of the Cross says, when we experience the 'ladder of love' we can do nothing that is not for the highest good for all concerned, including Source. The mystic Alice Bailey, too, urges us to use the love ray in all healing work.[92] When we experience absolute love, all dualities and conflicts are diminished. We might conclude that stillness equals consciousness. But then we realize that consciousness is love and love is all. Romantic love makes it possible for us to experience this.[93]

Initiation of Illness

"The heart at rest sees a feast in everything." —
Hindi proverb

For most of us, illness is seen as something negative. We get a flu shot so we won't miss work. We send our kids to school even though they have a cold because childcare isn't available. Mental illness feels scarily unpredictable. Depression is misunderstood and denigrated, especially when there does not seem to be any ostensible reason to be depressed.

In some religions, we're told that when we get an illness it's punishment for some sin or other. Others explain it in terms of karma, and still others as being bad luck or bad genes. Or we're told we don't have the right attitude to ward off the illness, or that we attracted it into our lives—it's our fault we are sick.

But what if we regarded it as an initiation?

When we allow the reality of being ill to enter us, similar to the flow of energy the Taoists call *wu wei*, perhaps we could move with the illness, through the illness, and let the illness move through us.

What can we learn from illness? How can we transform ourselves and emerge wiser, more compassionate, and grateful?

Feeling fired up

For twenty years, Marcie had operated a successful, nonprofit art studio that she founded herself. The studio offered classes and opportunities for people of all ages and levels of experience to learn, as well as an exhibition and performance space. It was a huge blessing to the community that she lived in and loved, and it was her devoted passion since its inception.

But she'd had to endure one apparent setback after another. Each disastrous event, including a major plumbing catastrophe in the building, seemed to mark the end of the art center itself. The final straw was a bout of pneumonia that left her unable to work for several weeks.

By the time she came to see me, her health was beginning to improve, but she was questioning whether or not the universe was sending a message that she was supposed to give up her dream of a successful art studio and instead do something else entirely.

"Do you think it's time for me to be doing something else?" she asked, restlessly.

A petite, energetic, woman, Marcie could hardly sit still, even though she looked exhausted. Her sparkle seemed dimmed. Her hands were constantly gesticulating, but the energy was scattered. I could see from her birth chart that she was definitely a "fire person," but at this point she appeared to be burnt out.

Often when a person is burnt out, the solution, I find, is to nourish them with the sweet stillness of emotional water. But this did not feel to be the case with Marcie.

What she needed was energetic fuel.

Getting into the stillness of a fire person can be difficult, because they are, by nature, not still. But I could see that Marcie needed to feel stillness in order to know what it was that she wanted to be doing with her life.

"Do you think I should be doing something else?" she asked again.

"Like what?"

She had plenty of options and suggestions herself, throwing each one out into the air between us like a struck match that quickly extinguished itself.

Perhaps she should explore her spirituality? Or be more creative herself—maybe go back to her old love, which was painting? Or is the message that she should give herself more "me time"? Or was it wise to spend more time with her family? She was in her mid-fifties and she and her husband would soon be empty-nesters.

But it seemed, based on the tone of her voice, that these were just flickers of ideas to her, without much energy behind them. And even sorting through them looked like it was exhausting her.

I advised her to take a break from all her ideas. We looked again at her horoscope to get a glimpse of the over-arching view of her soul—past, present, and future. We gazed at it in stillness for a brief while. The little glyphs on the page seemed to shimmer and sparkle—with a lot of energy in her tenth house of professional life and public service.

All the houses and planets that ruled motherhood, romance, family, and what-about-me energy were secondary. And there was so much fire in her chart I could practically hear it crackling—Marcie's energy and passion for her work were clearly boundless.

Her fiery Mars in Sagittarius, for instance, and the lovely Venus so creatively placed in the fifth house. All the classes she offered, the nonprofit business that was such a boon to the community, people of all ages who were helped by her fierce passion for art seemed to glow like a steady candleflame at the heart of her life's purpose.

"You need to use your fire to fire up other people," I told her, smiling. "There is nothing new that is happening here for you. You would never be happy if you didn't have your work to sink your teeth into. It *is* your life."

"Why is it so hard then?" she asked, looking relieved but puzzled. "Why do you think I got sick?"

I pointed out that her pneumonia was showing up as too much water in some planetary transits in her chart. The plumbing issue as well … I asked if she'd also had extra-emotional ups and downs the past few months. It turned out she had—there was a sibling issue around a will that had created a rift in the family and which was heartbreaking to her.

The watery world of emotions was not where Marcie felt most comfortable—she was happier when she was doing, accomplishing, and creating.

"Usually, when I see a lot of fire in a chart, I wonder whether there's a need for water," I told her, "but with you it seems to have drenched your spirit quite a bit already these past few months. You're soaked and discouraged. The supposed disasters have nothing to do with your life's purpose. You need to continue to do what you're doing. You need to put all your passion and energy toward your work, with commitment, enthusiasm, and confidence. It'll all go okay again for you. You'll see."

I watched her tired, intense face light up with relief. It continues to amaze me how often we know exactly what we want to be doing, but we are afraid we might be 'wrong' about it. When we are given 'permission' to do what our heart desires, more than any other emotion, we feel relief.

Marcie loves her family and she probably does need to take better care of herself, but what seemed like disasters to her business and career were not a wake-up call for her to do something entirely different, as she had feared. There is still plenty for her to accomplish and create, and I see a strong, beautiful future ahead for her in her life's work of growing her community art center.

The problem of pain

Pain—whether emotional or physical—is one of the most disturbing aspects of any illness. It is difficult to feel still when we are in pain. Pain induces overwhelming nerve sensations in our brains that make it almost impossible to focus on anything else.

When pain shows up as an initiation, it's a good time to have a conversation with the pain. Why is it there? What does it want you to know or understand? Everything shows up as an ally in our lives, even if it sometimes seems that can't possibly be so.

Sometimes it's too hard to tune into this on our own. A healing practitioner can help us to have this conversation. Healing doesn't take place until something has shifted in our psyche and our understanding about our suffering. Seek the help of a stillness touch practitioner or a healer who understands the value of stillness in helping you to overcome pain. Acupuncture, reiki, cranio-sacral, and energy healers who work in the realm of stillness can guide you to that time before your immune system kicked in and you were whole. In that stillness, pain disappears.

Being present with the illness or disease may be a way to move through it.

If we recall Einstein's words about all matter being energy, then we can look at health and healing in a more energetic way. Energy must flow, it has to keep moving. When it gets blocked or stuck we get sick. The main attribute of life is a constant birth, growth, deterioration, and death, and birth again.

Everyone's experience of illness is personal, and whatever initiation they experience through it is their own. I've encountered people whose lives were altered irrevocably through cancer and heart attacks, for instance. It wasn't so much that they changed their diet or lifestyle: it was that they changed their entire perspective on life.

What matters? Where do you want to put your energy? More importantly, where do you want to put your stillness?

I have yet to meet someone who experienced a severe illness who, after having recovered, said, "I want to work harder and do less of the things I enjoy." Or, "I'm not going to do all the things I had on my bucket list to do before I die." Or, "I'm going to devote myself to making money from now on." Or, "I want to sweat the small stuff now." Or, "I won't forgive."

Illness does not diminish us—it expands us.

Metaphysical Healing

Several years ago, I was driving into town to meet a friend when, suddenly, my vision blurred and doubled and I had to pull over to the side of the road. In front of me all I could see were two roads, two trees, two fences. Everything was doubled. Stupidly, I pulled back onto the road and tried to concentrate on the middle double lines as I drove. It was no use: the two bright yellow lines became four, then occasionally eight, sometimes even more, and they weaved and looped before me.

I hurriedly pulled over again and turned off the car's engine, wondering what to do.

At first, I assumed my sight was the problem, and, as is typical of me, heartily wished the issue would just go away without my having to do anything about it. It was Thursday, the weekend was coming, by Monday, I hoped, everything would be back to normal.

But my husband thought a doctor's visit was a good idea, so the next morning he drove me to a hastily made appointment. On learning what the problem was, there was a sudden scurry of activity. I was immediately sent to an ophthalmologist for an emergency eye exam.

She told me after the test that she had good news and bad news. "The good news is there is nothing wrong with your eyes," she said. "The bad news is there is nothing wrong with your eyes."

So, followed a strange weekend of more tests to learn what else might be the matter.

The test I remember most vividly was the MRI and the claustrophobic experience of being slid into this loud machine with all its hums and clanks and ticking. I also remember vividly the kindness from the technician who was taking me through the test. I've had friends who told me that when they'd had MRIs, the technician would usually reassure them afterward, even though that was their doctor's job. But this young man took my arm gently, and guided me back upstairs, without saying a word. I knew instinctively something was very wrong, beyond the continued double vision that confounded my sight.

I was summoned back to my doctor the next day. My husband drove me and logged into his computer in the waiting room. He was in the midst of a project when I was called into a room, so I went in alone, following the double image of the nurse who walked ahead of me. I was getting used to it by then.

"Your results came in from the MRI," the doctor stated, slowly.

And then she paused. I felt myself floating up to the ceiling and as I looked down I heard a voice (my own) asking calmly, "Should I bring my husband in to hear this?"

Even then I believed she would smile and shake her head and reassure me, but instead she paused again and then said, "Yes, I think that would be best."

Once my husband came in, she proceeded to tell me that they had found something serious in my brain that was causing damage to my optic nerves. They could not determine what it was without more tests.

"What are some of the possibilities?" I asked.

"You don't have other symptoms of stroke but it could be that. Or a tumor or the beginning of multiple sclerosis. We need to set up an appointment with a neurologist right away."

The next day, in the neurologist's office, I was told that in order to find out more about the source of the aberration, he would need to administer "a small puncture to the lumbar region" and examine my spinal fluid.

"You mean a spinal tap?" I said.

And my husband, who up till then had been admirably stoic, promptly fainted.

The spinal tap revealed that I had a Lyme infection that had somehow penetrated my brain and lodged there. Heavy antibiotics improved my health and my sight and by the end of that long summer I was back to 'normal.'

Unfortunately, because of the way Lyme disease works, I was infected with some form of it practically every year. I tried pretty much everything I could to prevent getting it, including wearing a gardening outfit with booties and mitts attached, similar to the outfits that people who clean up radioactive waste wear. For a couple of years, I hardly ventured into the garden at all, but stayed on walkways, roads, and inside.

I still got Lyme. Not in my brain again, but in ways that felt devastating. During each relapse, I'd forget what it was like to be well. I'd experience incapacitating and bone-deep aches and pains accompanied by hopelessness—these were just some of the symptoms. They were different each time.

Some years after that first episode, as I was undergoing my umpteenth round of doxycycline, a healer friend suggested that I explore the metaphysical aspect of Lyme. I had done so much research by this time, that I thought I had 'tried everything.'

But I hadn't tried making friends with it or asking it why it kept returning.

That summer, I spent long hours in a mystical conversation with the infecting spirochete. Why did it choose me? What was it trying to teach me? What was the lesson?

What is a tick? I wondered. What is it like? How

does it feed, procreate, and where does it proliferate and why? By exploring its physical characteristics I hoped I'd begin to understand its metaphysical message.

Ticks are parasites. The tick feeds off of its host. So what was happening in my life that made me feel like someone could feed off me? Was I feeling used or abused?

No, the parasite aspect didn't resonate with me. Nor was I drawn to the concept that they were "sucking the life-blood out of me" that someone mentioned. During the ten years I experienced recurring Lyme, I went through some of the most dramatic changes in my life: both my parents died, both my children grew up and forged their own lives in the world, and I left my high school teaching profession behind. I also began practicing full-time as a metaphysician.

I went on exploring inwardly. The tick injects something into the bloodstream. It's almost as though it's a reciprocal exchange of energy.

What is that about?

For several weeks, my meditations focused solely on my illness. The antibiotics were working, so I was starting to feel better—although weak—and I made a resolution that this was the last time I would ever get

Lyme.

I would hear whatever it was that was being said.

Here are excerpts from my journal during that time:

August 5

Last night I awoke from a nightmare. In my dream I was screaming, "Help me! Help me!"

As I settled into consciousness I felt overwhelmed with that helpless hopeless grief that penetrates your soul when it comes and you think you will die from sadness. I thought then too of the Lyme, since I'd asked for help in understanding it, and wondered if my Lyme is a cry for help.

And I wonder too if it touches on a very deep residue of depression that may still reside within me, almost as though it's trying to dig out the last vestige of depression within me, as though it's sucking it out like leeches were supposed to suck out infected blood back in the past.

I became intrigued by the possibility that my Lyme was digging feelings out from old, embedded layers. It was as though I were being cleansed, rather than infected.

Metaphysician Laura Bruno is in the process of writing a book called *The Metaphysics of Lyme Disease,* which I'm looking forward to reading, but in the

meantime her website offered some valuable insights
for me:

> "Lyme Disease tends to appear in people who could go
> even deeper with their healing and creative gifts but
> for one reason or another feel locked into their current
> lifestyle. Perhaps they have unexpressed creative gifts
> like photography, painting, or writing. Maybe they've
> been waiting for life to "let up" before they
> indulge such longings. ... Lyme seems to show up like
> a roto-rooter, forcing people to dig deep and remove
> ALL blocks to creativity and healing. To the outside
> world, these people usually look like they have no
> blocks because they're moving so effectively through
> life, but Life has other plans. It's as though these
> people came in with a bigger mission than their
> current lifestyle or world view allows. They may get
> nudged a few times, but if they don't respond fully,
> then along come some little spirochetes to terrorize the
> immune and neurological systems into action. Like a
> guerilla army, the bacteria sneak inside without
> detection and then launch a massive attack that
> captures attention through shock and awe."[94]

I opened myself to that shock and awe in a new
way. Instead of being horrified, I became interested —
not so much in the biology of Lyme, but in the
experience of Lyme.

The revelation came that perhaps Lyme was a gift,
a Roto-Rooter experience to root out the last of my
grief, from past lives, early childhood, and adult life,
as well as other people's grief, and the sadness of our
beautiful, brave planet earth herself. The sadness thus

became energy rather than illness.

I realized that when we love life and all that that entails, sadness is simply a part of it. It's neutral. But it had been out of balance in my psyche for as long as I could remember.

I never did contract Lyme again after that summer. My heart felt lighter too. I'm no longer afraid I'll be overwhelmed by sorrow because of all the suffering in the world and that I need to keep my feelings at bay. It's as though the Lyme helped me become fully integrated into myself. I'm gradually becoming more at home with my feelings, my longings, my reality, and my life.

Dementia

When my mother succumbed increasingly to the illness of Alzheimer's, it was as though she existed in a reality that was very different to the one we had known together up till then. Since she had little memory left, she became, paradoxically, still *and also* in the motion-moment.

What I mean by that is that she lived completely in the present.

She would look out the window and see a bird and become so animated and thrilled by the sight that

I would get excited too. I would tell her, "You've finally achieved living in the *now*! You've become a Zen master!" And she would laugh and laugh and say, yes, that is true.

After my mother was diagnosed with Alzheimer's, she lived the next five years, until she died, exploring the spiritual nature of her illness with great interest. She read Rudolf Steiner's *Cosmic Memory* for the umpteenth time and told me she had never understood it before.

But even three decades before she was diagnosed with Alzheimer's she was already interested in the problem of memory—or the lack of it. She wrote this in one of her unpublished books called "How to Begin":

"Memory—Black Holes.

We are like the night sky, thousands of millions of stars flickering up there in bright patterns. Among the stars, are also millions of black holes.

Black holes are huge places in the sky which suck in the vast amounts of matter and never spewing out. They are whirlpools of black space, everything goes in, nothing returns.

That's what our minds seems like nowadays. Full of black holes. These holes are where everything we were supposed to remember goes. Nothing seems to come back when we wanted.

We have a black hole for answering letters, for finding the keys, for returning borrowed books. For remembering to call someone, for paying the bills. For balancing checkbooks. For names, numbers, addresses. Even for appointments we want to keep.

What else is there? Whatever it is, we forgot.

Is it because we are growing old?

Let's look at this memory thing a bit more closely.

When you were younger, you simply forgot. I forgot, you said, watching in surprise at the anguished contortions of the adults at this crystal-clear explanation. Mothers, teachers, and even friends irritated the life out of you by constantly reminding you.

It was natural to forget. It happened all the time.

When you didn't bring home the groceries, "I forgot," you said, ridding yourself of all blame in the matter. When you left your jacket behind, "I forgot it," you said of the irretrievable object. You thought you were sweet, darling, forgivable to forget. You certainly weren't being mischievous, lazy, or passive-aggressive, much less senile.

If you couldn't remember a name, it was because you had forgotten to do your homework. Later on, your absent-minded habits seemed to be what made you endearing. If you lost your keys, your spouse loved you more, because it meant having to take care of you.

But after fifty, people think it's Alzheimer's disease.

What is memory? What can we know about it? Where is it located? Is it something like a liver or a stomach?

The first thing to realize is that there is no such thing as memory.

Memory is something you do, not something you have.

No one has yet said so, but it is an inescapable fact. You don't have a memory, like a robot has a floppy disk. The entire you is a memory machine. And your life is part of this function.[95]

If we regarded the illness of dementia not as a huge loss but as an extraordinary Zen-like experience of presence, how would we feel? If we allowed patients to feel security in the moment and wisdom instead of loss and bewilderment, what would happen? Could feelings of wholeness and well-being be experienced even by people who can't remember?

My mother perhaps died slowly, but what happened, as I saw it, was that her essential spirit was growing stronger and stronger through those last years of being loved and cared for by my father. Then when she did die it felt organic rather than a huge shedding of her physical body.

If we could let go of the idea that our brains represent who we are, and return to the sense that our heart is who we are, then we wouldn't be so disconcerted and upset when someone can't remember if you are their daughter or their mother. Who cares, as long as they love you and you love them?

Initiation of Death

> *"What will happen in your life if you accept the*
> *invitation to stillness cannot be known ... what can*
> *be known is you will have a larger capacity to truly*
> *meet whatever appears."* —Gangaji

The fifth initiation concerns the transformation from physical existence to a different, and possibly unknowable, form of energy.

Many years ago I read about a woman who had been in a bad car accident. She experienced a sensation of leaving her body and floating around the accident scene in confusion and panic. Then she was drawn to a stranger in a car parked nearby who was quietly praying for the unknown victim of the accident.

According to the article, the woman who was in the car crash did not die after all, and after a lengthy recovery, returned to the scene of the accident, determined to find the person who had so unexpectedly offered a haven of peace at a time of chaos and terror. It turned out that she was able to trace the stranger—I forget how—who told her that this is something she feels called to do whenever she encounters an accident or other difficult situation.

Perhaps she was a chaplain or nurse—I don't remember. But I do remember that the two became friends, and the gratitude felt by the woman in the car accident was immense.

Ever since that time, I have tried to respond to tragedies with a similar stillness and calm whenever I can. I'll light a candle, say a prayer, and imagine that the person who is suffering or who died is surrounded with calm stillness, love, and light. This helps to take me out of a well of suffering and grieving and makes me feel active in the journey of life and death.

I'm not saying that this is the way to be during a terrible moment. I'm offering it as an option to those who wish they could "do" something at times like this. Outrage or horror are not always appropriate or helpful. Being calm is more likely to be a healing salve to everyone around.

The Death Card

Death is a symbol for transformation. In the tarot, the Death card (number thirteen in the major arcana, which may be where the Western triskaidekaphobia originated) does not mean physical death, but the cycles of nature ... of life.

We can't have life without death—or spring

without winter, or fresh roses without the old blooms dying, or any other organic cycle of life that exists in nature.

In the tarot, the guidance might be regarding a letting go of the past. It may be time to move on. Very possibly something has come to an end.

Ruled by Saturn, the theme of timing and responsibility in the Death card carries a great weight with in, including discernment on what to let go and what to take with you. Seeing our lives as part of a greater cosmic whole is part of the process of letting go peacefully.[96],[97]

How long will I live?

Many people want to know how much longer they have to live. The unknown can be terrifying. We think knowing will make us feel more in control. But since the future exists only in potential—there's no predetermined story here for each person. Not knowing contains more freedom than knowing does.

One man, Dino, consulted with me as he headed into retirement after a lifetime of being an extremely busy and ambitious lawyer—and a heart attack. Dino looked much older than his age of sixty-six. He hadn't been ready for retirement. The heart attack forced it though, and he gave in. His face was gray and I got the feeling that his heart felt heavy.

I pressed and prodded for hints of hobbies, passions, longings perhaps from his childhood that could now be resurfacing.

Nothing emerged.

He claimed he wasn't depressed but also said he had nothing to live for. He wanted to know how many more years he had to fill up. He loved his wife, but she was busy with her friends and social engagements. Their kids were grown. Without his work he wasn't sure what he'd do.

"What if I promised you'd live to be ninety-nine?" I said. "What would you choose to do?"

"Well, if it were ninety-nine, I'd better start on a new career. I'd have to make some money, for one thing."

"How would you do that?"

"Well, I'd know that I have time to get something going."

"Like what?"

"I don't know!" He sounded deeply frustrated. "Anything. Teaching. Consulting. Writing. Something to do with law, of course. That's what I love."

That's what I love.

And there was the nugget, the signature of who he was, is, and always will be. He was someone who cared about the law and wanted to go on working.

"It doesn't matter if you live for one year, ten years, or thirty," I said firmly. "You need to get to work."

"But I'm not well enough. I'll just have another heart attack. That's what the doctors say."

"Your heart attack is your friend—it's telling you that you can work in a way that's different and even more fulfilling that you've ever imagined. Maybe you don't want to practice law, but instead open a consulting practice. Or maybe you'll find that you love to teach. But it's time for you to get back on your feet and go to work. Not the way you were working, but the way you would love to work."

Not waiting but watching

Just as life itself is existential, and needs to be experienced in order to know, so is death. Dino was not asking me when was he going to die, but how was he going to live?

I showed him that dying and living are the same. If work and law is what he lived for, then it was also what he needed to do till he died. But there were many forms that it could take for him.

The process of dying itself, which happens in one way or another from the moment we're born, is simply part of being alive.

During the harrowing, vital, and mystical experience of watching someone die we are not waiting for the moment but witnessing the experience.

We don't do it enough: witness the world, witness other peoples' experiences, and, most important of all, witness our own place in the world. It happens in stillness.

Bringing stillness into the process makes us all feel more at peace, not just the one who is dying, but friends and family too.

Summary

"In stillness the muddied water returns to clarity."
—Lao-Tsu

Through using these building blocks of stillness in the four bodies (physical, mental, emotional, spiritual), we are given a foundation from which to climb to great heights of integration and wholeness.

We can find out about past lives and early childhood, connect with our higher selves, and glimpse our future potentials.

Trauma can be healed, nervous-making mental chatter can be calmed, and intuition and innate wisdom can direct our lives.

We can experience healing from past wounds, forgiveness, freedom from suffering, and connect with our soul's purpose.

And, through their integration, the essential questions that every metaphysician asks—"Who am I? What am I? Where have I been? Where am I going?"—are revealed to us.

Integrating stillness into the four bodies creates an experience that ripples out into all experience. It is the way dowsers are trained to dowse for water.[98]

Stillness helps us to expand into our optimal potential.

Stillness helps to deepen our relationship to nature, spirit, development of human consciousness.

Through stillness, we experience the nature of Source in our parenthetical human existence.

IV. Beyond Stillness

---

*"Religion and ritual can be vehicles for entering
stillness. It says in Psalm 46:10, 'Be still, and know
that I am God.' But they are still just vehicles. The
Buddha called his teaching a raft: You don't need to
carry it around with you after you've crossed the
river." —Eckhart Tolle*

Although stillness is in no way a religion or matter
of faith, it also is not just a physical or metaphysical
state of being. It is more than that: stillness opens
us to the mystical and personal experience that
connects us to our innermost nature and to Source.

Stillness, as a spiritual opening, is an active verb
as much as it is a state of being. Enlightenment, for
most of us, is not a one-off experience. It is a growing

and developing state that we access in different moments throughout our lifetimes. These openings are more like the regressions and progressions of a spiral than to a strict line.[99]

To refer back to Charles Ridley's exploration of embryogenesis: each one of us can access the stillpoint that was our existence in the first two weeks after conception, by allowing ourselves to feel it. In the same way, spiritual development can be seen as an experience of 'allowing' rather than 'seeking after.' We return to a stillpoint so that we can allow inherent wisdom and knowing to enter us, rather than thinking we have to learn or access something that lies outside of our own spirit.

Letting in receptive *and* creative stillness (at the same time) enables spiritual growth and connection to Source.

Thus, if we understand Source as stillness, then stillness is also our consciousness. At the heart of our understanding and connecting with Source is our development of consciousness.

Awareness of our own consciousness is the transcendent, mystical, and vitally human experience that stillness lets us have: *to become aware of being aware*. Eckart Tolle says: "I am not my thoughts, emotions, sense perceptions, and experiences. I am not the content of my life. I am Life. I am the space in which all things happen. I am consciousness. I am the Now. I am."[100]

I believe that as human beings connected to Source, we have a responsibility to Source. We do not exist in innocent stillness, we exist in *conscious* stillness. That is the great gift *and* the great responsibility of being human.

This is why gratitude is such a vital human practice. Gratitude is not a childlike, polite, fairly unconscious "thank you." The power of practicing gratitude is that we are consciously aware of being grateful. This is what we can experience in stillness: awareness of our awareness of feeling grateful.

Our awareness of our gratitude for the natural world surrounding us, for instance, is, as Eckhart proposes, as important to nature as nature is to each one of us: "When you perceive and join with nature in the field of stillness, that field becomes permeated with your awareness. That is your gift to nature."[101] It is awareness itself that creates a symbiotic relationship between the human being, the world around us, and consciousness.

How often have you looked at a sunset and said, "I love that sky!" Or you listened to the radio and said, "I love that song!" But when you turn this gratitude around, and say, "The song loves me" or "the sea loves me," you allow the sea to love you or the forest to love you. A rich and revealing symbiotic relationship occurs.

The Gift of Surrender

This is how it happened for me: I was walking on the beach early one morning, contemplating the years past and the years that lie ahead. Filled with intense emotion, I focused on the steady rhythm of my bare feet on the cool sand. I then heard something—a voice, a feeling? I don't know. But I heard it distinctly. It said: "Listen to the waves." So, I stopped and listened—for many hours, it turns out. I heard the sound of the crashing water as though I was hearing it for the first time—all the subtleties of the waves, the booming roar of the ocean, the crashes, the whispers, the rustle of the foam on the sand, the sweeping in and the rolling out of so much water, the endlessness.

The process was like getting to know a strange language I had never heard before. I realized the waves were not individual entities: they speak for the ocean.

And this is what I distinctly heard the waves say, over and over: *We only want to love you. Let us love you.*

In that moment, the world shifted for me. Everything in the world longs to love us: the birds, the wind, the sky, people. You might think that you enjoy being loved by someone else, but imagine or remember the joy of you yourself being in love. And so with nature, or the sand under our feet, or the nose of a puppy: it all wants to love us, as much or even more than we love it.

In stillness, we allow our thoughts to love us, our bodies to love us, nature, Source—everything. In stillness, we surrender to that love. In stillness we understand that surrender is not giving up, but *giving* itself.

The sun surrenders to its orbit and the moon surrenders to its being a reflection in silver light. A flower surrenders to its own fragrance. A candle surrenders to being lit.

In stillness, we surrender to our light, our happiness, our fragrance, our beating heart, our breath, our fullest potentiality. We transcend the personal to arrive at the heart of our signature nature. We surrender to who we are, just as the acorn surrenders to becoming a mighty oak.

The essential signature of anything is revealed in

its nature and potential. Regarding plants, this includes color, shape, texture, scent, and more. In exploring animal totem spirituality, we examine the lifestyle, personality, mating habits, and habitat of the creature in order to understand its signature or spiritual meaning.

The same is true with each one of us. We each have a 'signature' that manifested at the moment sperm encountered egg and generated us as a living entity. Environment, DNA, and experience all contribute to who we become, but through stillness we remember and can grow into that essential nature within us that has always been there.[102]

Look at James Hillman's acorn again. Within that little item exists the potential of an enormous oak tree. Within each human being lies their own expansive unique potential. And therein lies our destiny.

The greater purpose of stillness is to experience this thriving. Aristotle uses the term *eudaimonia* to talk about happiness. While the word translates as *happiness*, it also means *flourishing* or *thriving* as human beings. And in order to thrive, according to Aristotle, we need to seek the greatest human good, which is complete in and of itself.

In other words, we seek the good for its own sake,

not for any other reason—certainly not for applause or reward. It is in seeking goodness for goodness's sake that we are happy and complete.

How?

Through stillness or, as Aristotle calls it, contemplation. It is through contemplation that we not only experience eudaimonia but *we are also aware of experiencing it.*[103]

To extend the meaning from *thriving*—or feeling complete in ourselves as we move through our soul's development to becoming increasingly our signature self—is the satisfying experience of living paradoxically in both movement and stillness at the same time.

"The curious paradox is that when I accept myself just as I am, then I can change,"[104] says noted transpersonal psychologist Carl Rogers, because it is only in that stillness of complete acceptance that we can experience the freedom to cocreate and manifest destiny. We are our Source and we become our Source.

Spiritual development occurs in stillness by allowing the fullest expression of our human potential to occur.

In stillness, we experience the mystical truth that we are all one, all connected to Source. Source is our divine stillness.

Through stillness we realize we can 'be' one with Source (verb) rather than feeling separate and seeking Source (noun).

Source is Consciousness. As quantum physicists assert nowadays, and as mystics have asserted for centuries, it is not possible to formulate the laws of quantum mechanics in a fully consistent way without references to consciousness.[105]

Understanding Source as consciousness, and experiencing the consciousness of our becoming and our being, illuminates the age-old search for the meaning of existence. Moses was instructed to "Be still, and know that I am God,"[106] not to go running around trying to find God.

The great revelation of stillness shows us that we do not have to seek Source. Source is already within us.

Source is All-That-Is, our universe, and our center.

What Is Next?

> *"Two atoms, once having encountered each other,*
> *will forever be connected or have an influence on*
> *each other, regardless of their location or distance*
> *from each other ... this implies what the mystic*
> *states: the universe is connected, there is no true*
> *separation, what occurs here may instantly have an*
> *effect on there." —Steven Harrison*

I believe that whether it is physical healing we seek, or mental health and well-being, or connection with our inner self, or an understanding and reuniting with Source, stillness is the way.

It is the stillpoint from which wellness can exist.

We have seen how we can arrive at this stillpoint by becoming aware of being aware. Paradoxically, stillness is experienced as being beyond physicality, thought, or feelings—and yet within them at the same time.[107]

Beyond physical stillness lies a rich and rewarding experience of *aletheia,* or presence, and through stillness one sees through the veils that conceal that presence. This can be done through meditation, walks in nature, focusing on the breath— practices that help to still the mental chatter that disturbs the serenity of one's own eternal stillness.

Beyond the stillness of the mind is the stillness of

the heart. What the heart knows is far more real and wise and all-seeing than what the mind can understand. In the heart lies innate knowing, through feelings of what is true and good.

Spiritual development is the development of consciousness, and can be experienced through stillness. Our soul's purpose can be known and understood. Humans grow into their soul's purpose.

Our task is to recognize our soul's purpose, to align with that, and to feel part of the innate pattern that fulfills us into our potential.

This is what we can experience in stillness. We transcend the personal; and in that transcendence the present is revealed. It is in stillness that we can realize there is no separation: spirit and nature are one. Each breath we take and each word we speak can lead to a path of spiritual development.

Stillness allows us to become aware of our essential nature and potential.

It allows us to become aware of the self as part of the 'all' or Source.

Finally, it allows us to become aware of being aware.

Being aware of being aware is one of the essential aspects of human experience and spiritual development.

We move beyond stillness to an extraordinary equilibrium of being and becoming, actuality and potentiality, just as light is both particle (noun) and wave (verb).

As more research is done on stillness, its positive effects and benefits will be increasingly proven.

Through integrating the healing powers of stillness using the four elements as a starting point, each one of us can be helped to (1) allow our own physical healing to occur, (2) overcome psychological behaviors that hold us back, (3) experience guidance from our intuition, and (4) unveil life's mysteries of the soul and spirit through spiritual development.

I thought I would limit myself to those four essential aspects of human and spiritual development, but what I discovered is that stillness permeates every single aspect of being human and our developing awareness.

In fact, stillness may be an intrinsic aspect of the evolution and the future of human consciousness. My contribution—the approach to experiencing stillness through the four bodies—is just a beginning—it is *a* way, it is not *the* way.

I believe it's possible that, with a greater understanding of stillness, we will attain a greater understanding of consciousness.

As we increasingly understand our human experience as being one of energy, then we can even think of ourselves as "energy transformers," as Steven Harrison suggests:

> The body is the meeting point of consciousness and reality, energy and matter, silence and mind … Physicists use the term "wave of probability" to describe the smallest elements of matter. These elements have quantifiable existence only upon observation. Until the point of observation, they have tendencies or probabilities, but no actuality.[108]

Does a tree falling in the woods with no one around to hear it make a sound? We debated this at length as children, to little avail, but quantum physics may have the answer. It seems that nothing exists without consciousness of it.[109]

This means that our developing consciousness is what is creating the world around us. The aboriginals called this world "The Dreaming." It was a belief in a single, flexible world rather than multiple worlds separate from reality. It implies a constant flow of life that is unbounded by time. People of the past do not die, but rather become one with the people of the present, as the aboriginal Arunta believe.

Their concept of 'dreaming' their way into existence is reminiscent of our current physicists' experiments showing that nothing exists without our conscious participation in it.[110]

The development of human consciousness lies in becoming increasingly aware of being aware, and perhaps even being aware of being aware that one is aware ... on into infinity.

The words remind me of 'beware,' and I'm taken back to Ridley's description of the self-realization mechanism that occurs in the embryo in order to ward off 'other' that was discussed earlier. In consciousness, being aware is stillness and the injunction to beware is motion—it's self-realization.

Yes, it also serves for survival, but now it could be seen as the development of 'be aware of aware ...' as it becomes part of our human development—of our consciousness. The consciousness of 'aware' and 'beware' in the practice of stillness allows duality to fall away and we become healthy and whole once again.

Much more work can be done to explore the extraordinary healing and liberating power of stillness. Excitement courses through me as I envision more avenues that need to be researched. We have barely begun to scratch the surface of how stillness can become part of our daily lives.

My hope is that stillness in our four elements can be used as frame from which to build a solid foundation for healing and personal development in clients, friends, and self.

Through integrating stillness in our lives, we become whole and integrated in ourselves. It's a way to see our signature nature and potential. Understanding our signature selves allows us to express ourselves creatively and to live in accordance with our fullest potentiality: unfettered, unlimited, and free.

Stillness can be our reality, as much as change is our reality. And the knowledge we gain through quantum physics will also affect what we know about stillness. The fact that we have come to a place of not only learning about how the universe works, but seeing how our consciousness *affects* how it works is thrilling.[111]

So let us continue the exploration of stillness in community, through initiations, by embracing paradoxical and creative thinking, sharpening our awareness of the development of consciousness, exploring enlightenment, and experimenting with practices that help us commune with Source.

I hope stillness becomes your passion, as it is mine.

How to Begin

When I'm asked, "Where do I begin," this is my reply:

Start where you are.

The place to begin is not a place of experience nor is it a place of knowledge.

It's the place of where your heart is.

What is your heart saying about where you are?

Listen to it.

Let it breathe, let it shine, let it beat.

Then ask: *What do I love to do?*

Listen.

Then ask: *Who do I love to be?*

You need to listen often, and differently, and once you are listening, listen more deeply, more lightly — but the messages are always the same:

Do what you love.

Be who you love.

Do what you do.

Be who you are.

Now, be still and become stillness itself.

Appendices

EXPLANATION of TERMS

What do we mean by spirit and spirituality?

The words "spiritual" and "spirituality" are subject to personal interpretation. In this book, when I use these words, I refer to our spirit, our life force. I believe that to be human is to be spiritual, and to be spiritual is to be human.

When the word "spiritual" is used, it is often meant to express something that is separate and distinct from our physical, day-to-day lives. Dictionaries tend to define spirituality as being concerned with the human spirit or soul as opposed to material or physical things. But spirituality has changed over the decades, especially with the holistic approach to psychology pioneered by people like C. G. Jung and psychiatrist Stanislav Grof. Our human spirit is inextricably connected with our physicality and psychology—it's difficult, if not impossible, to separate them.

So, I prefer the definitions (from the thirteenth century) that describe our "spirit" as the animating or vital principle in us. The Latin word *spiritus* can mean a breathing (respiration, and of the wind) or a breath. It can also mean the breath of a god, which is where the meaning of inspiration comes from. It's also our breath of life, related to *spirare*, or breathing itself.

If we regard spirituality as the breath of life, we see that there exists no duality, no separation.[112]

In my work, I set out to show how stillness can help us express our human spirit's fullest potentiality. Understanding our spiritual nature then becomes not a dualistic experience but a holistic one. It is in this holistic view of the human being, as a four-fold entity, that transpersonal psychology differs from both mainstream psychology (which tends to look at the mental body as the main source of disease) and spirituality (which tends to ignore the integrative aspect of being human and separates *divine* from *human*, in religious terminology).

What we may term "spiritual" traditions enhance their humanistic realities: sacred texts include injunctions on moral codes such as humility, kindness, and serving others. Although couched in religiosity, these are humanistic *and* spiritual ways to live. In other words, to be human is to be spiritual, and vice versa. To expand into our fullest human potential, our whole being needs to be allowed to grow, expand, and live in its fullest sense: physical, mental, emotional, to allow our spirit to flourish to its fullest potential.

Jung believed that "the healthiest spiritual aim, that is, the one of most benefit to the individual, is that of individuation—of trying to become more and more fully and truly who we essentially are."[113] Thus, spiritual development is also the development of the human individual.

One of the main goals in counseling is the integration of the individual, so that each person can, in their life, express their fullest potentiality. In Jungian terms, it means that we "become more and more of our own full self, having less of it projected or repressed or split off and denied."[114]

Individuation is akin to becoming undivided. Transpersonal psychology (transcending the persona, or mask, of the individual) combines psychology with spirituality in the sense that our spirit or spiritual nature *is* our fullest potential.

So, as a foundation to the work of stillness, I want to clarify that spirituality is not something outside or distinct from ourselves, or something that exists in a dimension different to the one we're in now. The spirit in the human being is part of who we are. In working with stillness, we can discover that there is no duality and no separation between being human and being spiritual.

What is our "Source" of life?

In addition to the words *spiritual* and *spirituality*, I use the word Source, with a capital *S*, to refer to All-That-Is.

There are many names for Source, in a wide variety of languages, religions, biographies, and experiences. If you are religious, you may want to translate Source as God or Allah. If you are a more science-oriented reader, imagine Source as energy. Metaphysicians use words like *awareness* or *consciousness*. The Sufis call on the "Beloved," Hindus name it "Brahman." William James refers to it as the "Divine." In the Jewish tradition, God has many names, and observant Jews are careful not to write or speak God's name without reverence. Spiritual teacher Byron Katie says her god is "Reality." Paramahansa Yogananda says God is "Stillness."[115] Dr. Leon Masters offers these mystical alternative names for God: "Infinite Mind, Higher Mind, Higher Consciousness, The Absolute, Mental Totality, Inner Reality, Ultimate Identity, Infinite Intelligence, Cosmic Mind or Consciousness, The Ultimate, The Highest Level of Consciousness."[116]

Whatever your name, sometimes the act of naming creates a feeling of separation. It presents a familiar—but outmoded—concept of duality. Our primal experience of dualism holds that we are not only separate from our self, and from the physical world, but that we are separated from our Source. The feeling of loss and loneliness can become acute at times! But in showing how stillness can unveil life's mysteries of the soul and spirit through spiritual development, the most profound of all the mysteries, the nature of Source itself, can be plumbed.

It is in stillness that we can perceive that there is nothing separating us from our Source.

Source means All-That-Is in the sense that we are all ultimately connected to the same Energy/God/Love ... or whatever you want to call the All-That-Is-Greater-Than-Us-Within-Us. We are not separate from it. Through existing in human form we are becoming more conscious of it.

My assumption in this work is that our 'Source' is conscious and seeks to become more conscious, just as individual humans do.

Aristotle conceived of God as the ultimate cause of all motion in nature, in life, as both the Prime Mover and the Unmoved Mover of the universe. He says, "The substance or form is actuality. According to this argument, then, it is obvious that actuality is prior in substantial being to potency; and as we have said, one actuality always precedes another in time right back to the actuality of the eternal prime mover."[117]

Even in *Physics*, Aristotle describes his proof for the existence of a Prime Mover, or God, using the laws of physics. He calls this the principle of motion and stationariness, or motion and motionlessness. He posits the existence and physical facts of stillness and change as this proof: "We have argued that there always was motion and always will be motion throughout all time, and we have explained what is the first principle of this eternal motion: we have explained further which is the primary motion and which is the only motion that can be eternal: and we have pronounced the first movement to be unmoved."[118]

The Source of our existence is proved, he claims, because nothing finite can cause motion in infinite time.

Thus, we have the Source of movement, we have the human being who is moved, and we have our physical world through which we are being moved.

To take that notion one step forward, in order to return to our connection with Source, we need to experience that primal stillness *before* we are moved.

In the same way, using the big bang theory to

explain the beginning of the universe, we continue to posit the question of what happened *before* the big bang?

According to the teachings of Kabbalah, the existence of both God and human beings does not depend on an external cause. Shokek says: "God (whom Aristotle would consider as the 'First Cause' or 'Cause of causes') is the cause of Himself without any dependency on any external cause, for He Himself is the Cause of everything. And man, who carries the eternal soul of the Divine, also does not have an external cause, for he is a spiritual entity whose Divine soul is essentially a part of God Himself." [119]

That being cleared up, then, in my work when I refer to Source, I mean *our* Source—our Nature. We can say, 'The kingdom of God is within you," as Jesus Christ did, and instead of wondering whether there's a little old man with a white beard inside our chest somewhere, or up above the clouds, like an extra organ, realize that, like energy, God is part of who we are.

As you'll find in the preceding chapters, the practice of stillness reveals that Source is a verb as well as a noun—as is each one of us. We are a *becoming* as much as we are *beings*.

Our entire concept of "I and Thou" dissolves in stillness; instead, development of consciousness can take its place.

So, when the word Source is used in this book, it refers to the paradoxical experience that we all have of being and becoming, at the same time. We are sourced, sourcing, and source, in one.

> *"Nothing in all creation is so like God as stillness."*
> —*Meister Eckhart*

What is transpersonal psychology?

*"In transpersonal counseling, ... we are guiding
clients to living toward their fullest expression of
their human potentiality." —Errol Weiner*

I received my doctorate degree in transpersonal counseling and for my dissertation I researched the nature of "transpersonal stillness" specifically, as it can be applied in metaphysical healing sessions. But the nature of transpersonal psychology cannot be understood as a straightforward therapeutic modality or a doctor's theory that can be neatly summed up. It encompasses all aspects of our psychological development throughout our lives.

Originally, transpersonal psychology grew out of a dissatisfaction many psychologists (including Jung) had with the classical Freudians and the behaviorists, who are trained to regard people according to the behavior of animals and environment.

Abraham Maslow was one of the first psychologists to part ways with this way of thinking, in part because he believed that human beings were made up of far more than just their instincts and environment. He thought it was equally important to explore the human qualities of love, personal freedom, morality, art, and religion, among other things.[120]

The precursor to transpersonal psychology was known as humanistic psychology. Instead of regarding a person's psyche as determined by environment, stimulus / response, and reward / punishment, the humanist psychologists believed that humans are also capable of being inner wisdom, self-understanding, and that they aspire to experience their full human potential.

Human beings, these new psychologists believed, were not just biological entities made up of base instincts but healthy functioning beings who needed to be concerned with human growth and potential. Psychologists Maslow and Anthony Sutich started the Association for Humanistic Psychology, which recognized the interrelatedness between the psyche and the physical body. This opened many new healing holistic modalities, including Gestalt therapy, bioenergetics, and craniosacral work.

In the late 1960s, the humanistic psychological movement expanded further to include what was referred to as the 'spiritual' aspect of human beings. Stan Grof describes this in his history of the movement: "The renaissance of interest in Eastern spiritual philosophies, various mystical traditions, meditation, ancient and aboriginal wisdom ... made it clear that a comprehensive and cross-culturally valid psychology had to include observations from such areas as mystical states; cosmic consciousness; psychedelic experiences; trance phenomena; creativity; and religious, artistic, and scientific inspiration."[121]

By the turn of the century, it had incorporated many traditions, including Asian, shamanic traditions, esoteric and gnostic systems, alchemy, Celtic mysticism, and Native American spirituality. In a 2018 article in *Noumenon: Newsletter for the Nondual Perspective*, the transpersonal psychologist John Davis points out that by now transpersonal psychologists "recognize and honor the astounding variety in the manifestations of being. We identify a number of dimensions of diversity, including race, culture, gender, age, sexual preference, social class, and so on. Ecopsychologists point also to the diversity of species and ecosystems. Our task is to honor the differences and eliminate bias and oppression in any of these dimensions."[122]

Transpersonal counselors and metaphysicians use various depth psychologies and holistic techniques to help clients live more mindfully, overcome trauma, and achieve their fullest potential as human beings.

These include "experiences of shamans and their clients, those of initiates in native rites of passage and ancient mysteries of death and rebirth, of spiritual practitioners and mystics of all ages, and individuals in psychospiritual crisis."[123]

We offer practical guidance as the compass on a client's journey, both in a humanistic loving way and in guiding the spiritual unfolding of their core being. It is "a whole-person, transformative approach to human existence and human experience that includes the spiritual and transcendent as well as the social and community dimensions of human life, all within the context of the global eco-system in which we live."[124]

A whole-person approach is at the fundament of healing. The word *heal* is rooted in the word *haelan*, which originally meant "whole." In order to feel whole, balanced, and healthy, a human being needs to be balanced physically, emotionally, mentally, and spiritually.[125]

Transpersonal psychology is an integrative and holistic psychology that understands "the human mind as interwoven with the fabric of body, community, and world—all four of these inextricably linked within a matrix of transformative process."[126]

Stillness can be used in this transformative

process, as it guides us to our self-actualization, allowing for our highest human potential.

When I consult with clients, I work with them holistically—as emotional, mental, physical, and spiritual beings. When a client comes to me with a question about a relationship, for instance, we look beyond the external factors that seem to inform the situation and dive into who *they* are and who *they* are becoming within the framework of the relationship.

Transpersonal psychology is an eclectic field that studies the transpersonal, or self-transcendent, and spiritual aspects of human experience. It attempts to integrate spirituality, psychology, and the individual's own human, experiential striving.

This integrative, holistic view of the human being is the premise that I use in order to show how the healing power of stillness can be used for healing and development, which is why I'm taking time to here to describe what I mean by it.[127]

Transpersonal psychology encompasses experiential, transformative, and evolutionary potential in all therapeutic work, including working with stillness.

಄

About the Author

Photo by Sarah Dinan

Every morning, **Winslow Eliot** begins her day with her stillness meditation, which she creates into an image to send to her subscribers and followers. The rest of her day is spent in writing, lecturing, teaching, and consulting. She is a teacher of tarot and intuitive arts; she lectures regularly on metaphysics, and she offers a popular weekly tarot master class in upstate New York. She is a Waldorf teacher, a mentor for writers, and she has certifications and diplomas in hypnotherapy, angels, mediumship, crystal healing, and Waldorf education. As a metaphysical practitioner, she uses the tarot, hands, stars, and the heart energy that flows between querent and reader to balance, center, and encourage her clients, many of whom return again and again.

Eliot is also an award-winning author. She has published a dozen novels (St. Martin's Press 1993; several romances published by NAL/Signet), a book of poetry, and a spiritual nonfiction book *What Would You Do If There Was Nothing You Had To Do? Practices to create your life the way you want it to be,* which won three awards in spirituality and self-help categories. She has also written many articles and a book on writing and mentoring writers (*Writing through the Year*).

An ordained interfaith minister in the International Metaphysical Ministry, she earned her PhD in Transpersonal Counseling from the University of Sedona. Currently, she writes, consults, and teaches in the Berkshires of western Massachusetts. You can get in touch with her or sign up to receive her *Daily Stillness* through her website: winsloweliot.com.

Acknowledgments

I am grateful for my many mentors, teachers, students, and friends who have helped me to shape this endeavor; most especially to my parents, who introduced me to the ancient Greek thinkers and philosophers in particular; Jesse Darrell, Francesca Margulies, and Jean Zay who opened me to Rudolf Steiner's insights; Dr. Neal Brogden, for the philosophies of Hegel and Nietzsche; Fred Paddock for helping me make friends with the work of Martin Heidegger, among many others; Gerald Born for opening my eyes to tarot, energy, and metaphysics in ways I'd never imagined; Eckhart Tolle for all his contributions to this important topic, as well as many, many other writers and thinkers, far too numerous to mention. The International Metaphysical Ministry, the Center for Anthroposophy, and the community at Stillness Speaks, as well as the community at the Association for Transpersonal Psychology, Lynda R. Exley and all my other advisors and mentors at the University of Sedona, thank you all so much for your invaluable research and generosity. Thank you to Nancy Crompton, Jefferson Eliot, and May Paddock for your patient, insightful, and wise comments as well as your editing expertise all the way through the writing of both the dissertation and the book itself. Thank you also to Laura Didyk for the thorough and valuable edit of the final version. And enormous gratitude to Tom Stier and Claudia Jackson, without whose constant encouragement I am lost. I am always grateful to my students, clients, and friends who continue to open me to the healing wonder and power of stillness.

References and Bibliography

Aristotle. *Metaphysics*. (W. D. Ross, Trans.). n.d. The Internet Classics Archive. http://classics.mit.edu. Retrieved 2018

Aristotle. *Nicomachean Ethics*. (W. D. Ross, Trans.). n.d. The Internet Classics Archive. http://classics.mit.edu. Retrieved 2018

Aristotle. *Physics*. (R. P. Hardie and R. K. Gaye, Trans.). n.d. The Internet Classics Archive. http://classics.mit.edu. Retrieved 2018

Bailey, Alice A. *Esoteric Healing. Volume IV: A Treatise on the Seven Rays.* New York City: Lucis Publishing Company, 1998

Barnett, Libby. *Reiki Energy Medicine: Bringing Healing Touch into Home, Hospital, and Hospice.* New York City: Healing Arts Press, 1996

Becker, Rollin E. *The Stillness of Life*. Hereford, UK: Stillness Press Llc, 2000. Retrieved from stillnesspress.com and ortho-bionomy.org. Web. 2018

Blackburn, Stewart. *It's Time to Come Home – With Kindness and Compassion We Come Back to Ourselves.* Hawai'i: Createspace, 2018

Blackburn, Stewart. *The Skills of Pleasure: Crafting the Life You Want.* Hawai'i: Createspace, 2013

Brach, Tara. *Radical Acceptance*. New York City: Bantam Dell. 2003

Buryn, Ed and Mary K. Greer. *The William Blake Tarot: Of the Creative Imagination.* Nevada City, CA: TAROT, 1995

Carse, David and Terence Stamp. *Perfect Brilliant Stillness.* Saline, MI: McNaughton & Gunn, 2005

Cousineau, Phil. *The Art of Pilgrimage—the seeker's guide to making travel sacred.* Newburyport, MA: Conari Press, 2012

Cowan, David Ian. *Seeing Beyond Illusions: Freeing Ourselves from Ego, Guilt, and the Belief in Separation.* Newburyport, MA: Weiser Books, 2015

David Chadwick. *Crooked Cucumber: The Life and Zen Teaching of Shunryu Suzuki.* New York City: Broadway Books, 1999

Deng, Ming-Dao. *Everyday Tao: Living with Balance and Harmony.* New York: HarperOne, 1996

Eliot, Ethel Cook. *The House Above the Trees.* London, UK: Thornton Butterworth, 1921

Eliot, Ethel Cook. *The Wind Boy.* New York City: Doubleday, 1925

Eliot, Winslow. *An Oasis for Writers: Writing through the Year.* Alford, MA: Writespa Press, 2011

Eliot, Winslow. *What Would You Do If There Was Nothing You Had to Do?* Alford, MA: Writespa Press, 2012

Ellwood, Robert. *Finding the Quiet Mind.* Wheaton, IL: Quest Books, 1983

Emoto, Masaru. *The Hidden Messages in Water.* Atria Books; September 20, 2005

Fallon, Bernie. *Goodology – Personal Development through Good*. Phoenix, AZ: Good Zone, 2011

Fadiman, James and Robert Frager (editors). Foreword by Huston Smith. *Essential Sufism*. New York: HarperOne, 1999

Frantzis, Bruce. *The Great Stillness: The Water Method of Taoist Meditation* Series. Berkeley, CA: North Atlantic Books, 2001

Friedman, Harris L., and Hartelius, Glen, editors. *The Wiley Blackwell Handbook of Transpersonal Psychology*. Chichester, UK: John Wiley & Sons, 2015

Girardot, N. J. *Myth and Meaning in Early Taoism*. Berkeley & Los Angeles, CA: University of California Press, 1974

Gohman, Julie. Book review of "Silence: The power of quiet in a world full of noise" by Thich Nhat Hanh. *The Journal of Transpersonal Psychology*, 2015, Vol. 47, No. 2. Web. May 30, 2018

Greene, Liz, and Juliet Sharman-Burke. *The Mythic Tarot*. New York City: Simon and Shuster, 2001

Grof, Stanislav. *A Brief History of Transpersonal Psychology*. Retrieved from stanislavgrof.com. n.d. Web. May 29, 2018

Hanson, Rick Ph.D. "Find Stillness." *Psychology Today*. Mar 24, 2014. Web. June 2, 2018

Harrison, Stephen. *Doing Nothing—Coming to the End of the Spiritual Search*. New York: Tarcher/Penguin Putnam, 1997

Hartelius, Glenn, Mariana Caplan PhD, & Mary Anne Rardin MA. "Transpersonal Psychology: Defining the Past, Divining the Future." *The Humanistic Psychologist*, Vol. 35:2. 2007

Harvey, John. *The Stillness of the Living Forest: A Year of Listening and Learning*. Brunswick, ME. Shanti Arts Publishing, 2018

Heidegger, Martin. *On Time and Being*. Trans. By Joan Stambaugh. Chicago and London: University of Chicago Press, 2002

Hillman, James. *The Soul's Code*. New York: Ballantine Books, 2017

Hoff, Benjamin. *The Tao of Pooh*. New York: Penguin Books. 1983

Iyer, Pico. *The Art of Stillness: Adventures in Going Nowhere*. New York: Simon & Schuster, 2014

James, William. *Varieties of Religious Experience*. New York: Penguin Classics, 1982

Johnson, Julie Tallard. *The Thundering Years: Rituals and Sacred Wisdom for Teens*. New York City: Bindu Books, 2001

Jung, Carl. *Collected Works*: The Tavistock Lectures, Vol XVIII. Retrieved from Google books. Web. August, 2018

Katie, Byron. *Loving What Is – Four Questions that Can Change Your Life*. New York City: Harmony Books, 2002

Kauffman, Joseph P. *Stillness: A Guide to Finding Your Inner Peace*. Conscious Collective, 2015

Keats, John. *The Complete Poetical Works and Letters of John Keats*. Boston, MA: Houghton, Mifflin & Co, 2012

King, Serge Kahili. *Mastering Your Hidden Self: A Guide to the Huna Way: A Guide to the Huna Way*. Wheaton, IL: Quest Books, 1985

Klein, Jean. *The Book of Listening*. Salisbury, UK: Nonduality Press, 2008

Long, Christopher P. *Aristotle on the Nature of Truth*. New York City: Cambridge University Press, 2011

Long, Max Freedom. *The Secret Science Behind Miracles*. Camarillo, CA: DeVorss and Co., 1986

Lovejoy, Arthur O. *The Revolt Against Dualism: An Inquiry Concerning the Existence of Ideas. The Paul Carus Lectures-Series 2*. La Salle, IL: The Open Court Publishing Company, 1960

Lynne, Carole. *Consult Your Inner Psychic: How to Use Intuitive Guidance to Make Your Life Work Better*. Newburyport, MA: Weiser Books, 2005

Mahler, Richard. *Daily Gifts of Solitude*. Newburyport, MA: Red Wheel/Weiser), 2003

Marko Pogacnik. *Nature Spirits & Elemental Beings: Working with the Intelligence in Nature*. Findhorn, Scotland: Findhorn Press, 1997

Maslow, Abraham H. *The Farther Reaches of Human Nature*. New York City: Penguin Books, 1971

Masters, Dr. Leon. *Mystical Insights—Knowing the Unknown*. Sedona, AZ: University of Sedona Publishing, 2016

Milne, A.A. *The World of Pooh*. London, UK: Methuen & Co, 1966

Moore, Ruth. *Niels Bohr: The Man, His Science, & the World They Changed*. New York City: Alfred A. Knopf, 1966

Mundy, Jon. *A Course in Mysticism and Miracles: Begin Your Spiritual Adventure*. Newburyport, MA: Weiser Books, 2018

Nhat Hanh, Thich. *Silence: the Power of Quiet in a World Full of Noise*. New York: HarperOne, 2016

Olsen, Brad. *Modern Esoteric: Beyond Our Senses*. (Series: The Esoteric Series Book 1) San Francisco, CA: CCC Publishing, 2017

Pagels, Heinz R. *The Cosmic Code: Quantum Physics as the Language of Nature*. Mineola, NY: Dover Publications, 1992

Pickett, Kathi. *On Becoming You*. Carlsbad, CA: Balboa Press, 2019

Pogacnik, Marko. *Nature Spirits & Elemental Beings: Working with the Intelligence in Nature*. Forres, UK: Findhorn Press, 2010

Reeves, Paula M., PhD. *Heart Sense: Unlocking Your Highest Purpose and Deepest Desires*. Newburyport, MA: Conari Press, 2003

Richman, Jana. *Finding Stillness in a Noisy World*. Salt Lake City, UT: University of Utah Press, 2018

Rivera, Maria. *Fly High!: A far-from-typical guide to get unstuck, regain hope, and seek new possibilities*. Prescott, AZ: Maria Rivera, 2018

Ridley, Charles. *Stillness: Biodynamic Cranial Practice and the Evolution of Consciousness*. Berkeley, CA: North Atlantic Books, 2006

Rogers, Carl. *On Becoming a Person*. New York: Houghton Mifflin, 1961

Roth, Bob. *Strength in Stillness: The Power of Transcendental Meditation*. New York: Simon and Schuster, 2018

Rothenberg, Albert. "The Process of Janusian Thinking in Creativity." *Archives of General Psychiatry*. 1971. Web. July 19, 2018

Sarno, John. *Healing Back Pain, Healing Back Pain: The Mind-Body Connection*. New York City: Grand Central Publishing, Hachette Book Group, 1991

Scheffel, Bill. "Meditation & Divination: A Review of the Taoist I Ching." Book review on Buddhist Portal. Web. August 31, 2016. Web. June 24, 2018

Schillings, Astrid. "Stillness and Awareness from Person to Person." *Focusing.org*. 2012. Web. July 14, 2018

Selbie, Joseph and Amit Goswami, PhD. *The Physics of God: Unifying Quantum Physics, Consciousness, M-Theory, Heaven, Neuroscience and Transcendence*. Newburyport, MA: New Page Books, 2017

Sfekas, Stanley. *Aristotle's Concept of God*. Indianapolis, IN: University of Indianapolis Press, 2015 10.13140/RG.2.1.1773.4483 Web

Shea, Michael J. *Biodynamic Craniosacral Therapy, Vol 3: Basic States of Stillness*. Berkeley, CA: North Atlantic Books, 2010

Shokek, Shimon. *Kabbalah and the Art of Being: The Smithsonian Lectures.* New York City: Routledge, 2001

Sion, Avi. *In Defense of Aristotle's Laws of Thought.* Geneva, Switzerland: Avi Sion, 2008

Sleigh, Julian. *Thirteen to Nineteen – Discovering the Light.* Edinburgh, Scotland: Floris Books, 1982

Solovyov, Vladimir. *The Meaning of Love.* Introduction by Owen Barfield. Hudson, NY: Lindisfarne Books, 1985

Steindl-Rast, Brother David. *Gratefulness, The Heart of Prayer: An Approach to Life in Fullness.* Ramsay, NJ: Paulist Press, 1984

Steiner, Rudolf. *Background to the Gospel of St Mark. Thirteen lectures given in Berlin, Munich, Hanover, and Coblenz, between 17 October, 1910 and 10 June, 1911.* London: Rudolf Steiner Press, 1968

Steiner, Rudolf. *Observations on Adolescence.* Fair Oaks, CA: AWSNA Press, 2001

Thurman, Robert. *Inner Revolution: Life, Liberty, and the Pursuit of Real Happiness,* 1998

Thurman, Robert. *The Tibetan Book of the Dead: The Great Book of Natural Liberation Through Understanding in the Between.* New York City: Random House, 1994

Tolle, Eckhart. *Stillness Speaks.* Novata, CA: New World Library, 2003

Tolle, Eckhart. *The Power of Now.* Novato, CA: New World Library, 1999

Weber, Gary and Richard Doyle. *Into the Stillness: Dialogues on Awakening Beyond Thought.* Oakland, CA: Nonduality Press, 2015

Weiner, Errol. *Transpersonal Astrology*. Dorset, UK: Element Books Ltd, 1991

Wilber, Ken. *The Atman Project: A Transpersonal View of Human Development*. Wheaton, IL: Quest Books, 1996

Wilhelm, Richard, trans. *The I-Ching or Book of Changes*. The Richard Wilhelm Translation rendered into English by Cary F. Baynes. Foreword by C.G. Jung. London: Routledge & Kegan Paul Ltd, 1971

Wong, Eva. *Cultivating Stillness: A Taoist Manual for Transforming Body and Mind*. Boulder, CO: Shambhala Press, 2012

Wrathall, Mark A. *Heidegger and Unconcealment: Truth, Language, and History*. New York City: Cambridge University Press, 2011

Wright, Patricia C., and Richard D. Wright. *The Divining Heart: Dowsing and Spiritual Unfoldment*. Rochester, Vermont: Destiny books, 1994

Notes

¹ On 1 March 1933, Carl Jung spoke about the tarot during a
seminar he was conducting on active imagination: "These
cards are ... psychological images, symbols with which one
plays, as the unconscious seems to play with its contents.
They combine in certain ways, and the different
combinations correspond to the playful development of
events in the history of mankind. The original cards of the
Tarot consist of the ordinary cards, the king, the queen, the
knight, the ace, etc, ... and besides, there are twenty-one
cards upon which are symbols, or pictures of symbolical
situations. For example, the symbol of the sun, or the
symbol of the man hung up by the feet, or the tower struck
by lightning, or the wheel of fortune, and so on. Those are
sort of archetypal ideas, of a differentiated nature, which
mingle with the ordinary constituents of the flow of the
unconscious, and therefore it is applicable for an intuitive
method that has the purpose of understanding the flow of
life, possibly even predicting future events, at all events
lending itself to the reading of the conditions of the present
moment. It is in that way analogous to the I Ching, the
Chinese divination method that allows at least a reading of
the present condition. You see, man always felt the need of
finding an access through the unconscious to the meaning
of an actual condition, because there is a sort of
correspondence or a likeness between the prevailing
condition and the condition of the collective unconscious."
From *Visions: Notes of the Seminar given in 1930–1934* by C.
G. Jung, edited by Claire Douglas. Vol. 2. Princeton NJ:
Princeton University Press, Bollingen Series XCIX, 1997), p
923

[2] The transpersonal psychologist John Davis describes this experience of stillness as "the mind, as a brilliant, luminous, crystal clear manifestation of Being, dissolves into Mind, and the moment unfolds. We feel intimate, vulnerable, graceful, alive, and blessed. Intellect becomes another expression of love and joy." From an article called "We Keep Asking Ourselves, What Is Transpersonal Psychology?" in *Nonduality*. Reprinted from *Noumenon: Newsletter for the Nondual Perspective*.

[3] Kriebel, Amanda. "Shavasana—Rest in Stillness." *Awareness Physical Therapy*. June 24, 2015. Web.

[4] In Julie Gohman's excellent book review of *Silence: The Power of Quiet in a World Full of Noise* by Thich Nhat Hanh, we see how 'Radio Non-Stop Thinking' can blemish our inward peacefulness. I explore this more in this book's chapter on *Air—Stillness in the Mental Body*. Gohman's review can be found in *The Journal of Transpersonal Psychology*, 2015, Vol. 47, No. 2.

[5] I love this description of time from tarot reader and author Jenna Matlin: "I do not think time is a train on a track and we are using tarot to glimpse the next three cities on this hard rail that cannot be altered. For me, tarot is the binoculars that looks up into a tree; stems and branches peeling away and diverging, growing, and moving where the future and the present intricately linked." —Jenna Matlin, blog post: "But I already knew that." 7/10/2017 queenofwandstarot.net

[6] This excerpt and musings on time are enriched by ideas from my old classmate Tobias Kaye, the founder and creator of Heart Sounding Bowls, in a post I came across called "Nailing the idea of Time in Four Levels of Reality." In it, he describes the nature of time through picturing Rudolf Steiner's fourfold human 'bodies'—the etheric (present/physical), astral (future/emotional), and spiritual (everywhen). He writes: "It's as though time stands still in the world of action—the present world in which we exist in the moment." Using the example of physically

hammering a nail home, which outwardly appears to be linked to a linear time (cause and effect), Kaye explains how an action learned over many years becomes part of the etheric body, or the physical flow of our eternal knowing. The flow of action comes from a place 'beyond simple intention' and is not related to feelings or thoughts, but to action. These skills live in our etheric body and they are always there once you've got them. ... That is timelessness in our etheric body. The emotional (astral) or airy body of our inner wisdom, Kaye says, experiences time flowing backward, from the point of completion into the experience of doing. We only engage in the act because we visualize it already completed. We act out of the objective of the deed. "Time flows backward in the astral world of thoughts and feelings." The spiritual world exists in timelessness, because whether or not something has happened yet—or not—does not affect anything. In the spiritual world all things already are, whether they have happened yet or not does not affect them. This is because the intention or purpose for hammering or nailing exists before we've even begun. We know what we plan to do, we may have even gotten plans from an existing book shelf. "What you are building already exists in potential and elsewhere. Time in the spiritual world already encompasses all things." *Sounding Bowls.* Facebook post, May 17, 2017.

7 Hillman, James. *The Soul's Code.* New York: Ballantine Books, 2017, p 7.

8 According to Aristotle in *Physics*, everything that is alive has within it "a principle of motion and of stationariness (in respect of place, or of growth and decrease, or by way of alteration). Aristotle. *Physics.* (R. P. Hardie and R. K. Gaye, Trans.). n.d. Book II, part 1

9 Aristotle describes the nature of existence as being motion and stillness, and, with his inimitable logic, shows it to be a combination of matter and form: "What is still weather? Absence of motion in a large expanse of air; air is the matter,

and absence of motion is the actuality and substance. What is a calm? Smoothness of sea; the material substratum is the sea, and the actuality or shape is smoothness." Using Aristotle's analogy, a person is the matter and their life is their essence or form. Combine the two, and we have a developing human being. *Ibid*, Book VIII, part 2

[10] James Hillman uses the analogy of the acorn and the oak in his insightful book, *The Soul's Code*. "The acorn grows into an oak, with a pre-set, unique image and pattern that unfold regardless of race, gender, parents, socio-cultural status, environment, nature or nurture ... Each person bears a uniqueness that asks to be lived and that is already present before it can be lived." Hillman, p 9

[11] One of my favorite forays during my research was into Stephen Harrison's small but intense book called "Doing Nothing." As a non-physicist, I was enlightened on the basic concepts of quantum physics in thrilling ways. Harrison outlines the connections between mysticism and science very satisfactorily, in my opinion. "Science knows little about the attributes of Consciousness. Only archetype and mythology have attempted to describe the conscious Universe, in which exists the answers to the mysteries of disease, aging, and death. But, each of us has the capacity to connect myth and science, physics and metaphysics, the material and the mystic. This connection is our birthright—it is the very nature of existence." Harrison, Stephen. *Doing Nothing—Coming to the End of the Spiritual Search*. New York: Tarcher/Penguin Putnam, 1997. Print. p 119–20

[12] Harrison, p 120

[13] Tam Hunt on December 5, 2018 *Scientific American*, "The Hippies Were Right: It's All about Vibrations, Man! A new theory of consciousness." One of Hunt's suggestions regarding consciousness is that all things are conscious, to some degree: "Based on the observed behavior of the entities that surround us, from electrons to atoms to molecules to bacteria to paramecia to mice, bats, rats, etc., all things may be viewed as at least a little conscious. This

sounds strange at first blush, but "panpsychism" — the view that all matter has some associated consciousness — is an increasingly **accepted** position with respect to the nature of consciousness."

14 Osteopaths and craniosacral practitioners like Becker, Ridley, and Shea have researched the powerful force of stillness extensively and also believe that it is when we are return to our original still state that physical healing and well-being can occur. They have discovered that it is through allowing our true nature (which is stillness) to express itself, we experience well-being. Becker, Rollin E. *The Stillness of Life.* Hereford, UK: Stillness Press Llc, 2000. Retrieved from stillnesspress.com and ortho-bionomy.org. Web.

15 Ridley, Charles. *Stillness: Biodynamic Cranial Practice and the Evolution of Consciousness.* Berkeley, CA: North Atlantic Books, 2006. Ebook. Ch 1.

16 Shea, Michael J. *Biodynamic Craniosacral Therapy, Vol 3: Basic States of Stillness.* Berkeley, CA: North Atlantic Books. 2010. p 386

17 Charles Ridley writes: "Self-recognition is our identity — the capacity for self-awareness — and it's the foundation of our perceptual integrity, which includes perception, response, and learning." Ridley, ch 1

18 Michael J. Shea writes in *Biodynamic Craniosacral Therapy, Vol 3: Basic States of Stillness.* Berkeley, CA: North Atlantic Books. 2010. p 386: "It feels like a filter has been removed from the senses. Even one's vision feels very clear. The stillness seems to be everywhere all at once or nonlocal, without a fulcrum of orientation. It simply is. ... One is aware of the stillness and part of it at the same time." Or, he goes on, we may notice "localized states of quiet, silence, a stillpoint, a pause, idling, and/or stillness in the client or in the practitioner himself. This is an embryonic or metabolic stillness."

19 Gendlin, too, writes of "times late in therapy when there is suddenly a clearer perception. The world seems poignant and sharply etched; it is as if the windows had just been

washed—one sees the same things as before, but what a difference! ... At such times experience is vastly better than all the meanings in one's perceptual set." Quoted in Schillings, Astrid. "Stillness and Awareness from Person to Person." *Focusing.org.* 2012. Web. n.p.

[20] When we allow our bodies to experience a physical stillness we experience relief from physical trauma or pain. After having written *Life in Motion*, the osteopath Dr. Rollin E. Becker wrote *Stillness of Life*, in which he describes his healing method of stimulating inner awareness to awaken within the individual a sense of natural balance and well-being through stillness. "The inner wisdom of the body is recognized and affirmed. Self-healing occurs as the person remembers their natural ability to move away from pain and toward ease." Becker, Rollin E. *The Stillness of Life.* Hereford, UK: Stillness Press Llc, 2000. Retrieved from stillnesspress.com and ortho-bionomy.org. Web. n.p.

[21] Quoted in *The Amen Vibration*, Volume 2 by Richie Quirino

[22] Jenny, Hans. *Cymatics : a study of wave phenomena and vibration.* Newmarket, NH : MACROmedia, 2001l. An overview of the pioneering work done by Dr. Hans Jenny with audible vibration on various substances. His research had led to speculation about the origin of matter and its relation to vibration and sound. From cymaticsource.com: "Cymatics, from Ancient Greek: κῦμα, meaning 'wave,' is a subset of modal vibrational phenomena. Typically the surface of a plate, diaphragm or membrane is vibrated, and regions of maximum and minimum displacement are made visible in a thin coating of particles, paste or liquid. Different patterns emerge in the excitatory medium depending on the geometry of the plate and the driving frequency." ... "Dr. Hans Jenny's cymatic images are truly awe-inspiring, not only for their visual beauty in portraying the inherent responsiveness of matter to sound (vibration) but because they inspire a deep recognition that we, too, are part and parcel of this same complex and intricate vibrational matrix – the music of the spheres!

These pages illumine the very principles which inspired the ancient Greek philosophers Heraclitus, Pythagoras and Plato, and cosmologists Giordano Bruno and Johannes Kepler."

23 Olsen, Brad. *Modern Esoteric: Beyond Our Senses.* (Series: The Esoteric Series Book 1) 2nd Edition. CCC Publishing; 2 edition (September 18, 2017). p 367

24 Ibid, in which he quotes *The Amen Vibration, Volume 2* by Richie Quirino: "The universe is made up of radiating energy vibrating at a multitude of varying frequencies and affects everything animate and inanimate. ... Studies reveal that 432 Hz tuning vibrates with the universe's golden mean PHI and unifies the properties of light, time, space, matter, gravity and magnetism with biology, the DNA code and consciousness. When our atoms and DNA start to resonate in harmony with the spiraling pattern of nature, our sense of connection to nature is magnified."

25 Ingrid Fetell Lee presented "Where joy hides and how to find it" at a TED conference in 2018. She states: "Cherry blossoms and rainbows, bubbles and googly eyes: Why do some things seem to create such universal joy? In this captivating talk, Ingrid Fetell Lee reveals the surprisingly tangible roots of joy and shows how we all can find—and create—more of it in the world around us."

26 Annabel O'Neill is a certified forest therapy healer and forest bathing expert, as well as an expert in many other things: writing, astrology, building her own tiny house, created a lifestyle company and clothing line, and world traveler. You can learn more about her work here: https://www.annabeloneill.com/. Her forest therapy work was featured on *CBS News This Morning*.

27 Haile, Rahawa. "Forest Bathing: How Microdosing on Nature Can Help With Stress." *The Atlantic.* June 30, 2017.

28 Tolle, Eckhart. *Stillness Speaks*, ch 7

29 Wrathall, Mark A. *Heidegger and Unconcealment: Truth, Language, and History.* New York City: Cambridge University Press, 2011. Print. p 13. "One key feature of

Dasein's being—one of the things which makes us the kind of entities we are—is that we understand our being and thus are able to comport ourselves toward it. ... When a tree grows, it neither reaffirms nor calls into question its being as a living thing—it just is what it is. But everything we do either reinforces or undermines the way we live in the world."

[30] Tolle, *Stillness Speaks*, ch 7

[31] Qtd. Julie Gohman's book review of *Silence: The Power of Quiet in a World Full of Noise* by Thich Nhat Hanh. The Journal of Transpersonal Psychology, 2015, Vol. 47, No. 2. Web.

[32] Katie, Byron. *Loving What Is – Four Questions that Can Change Your Life*. Harmony Books: NYC. 2002. p 5

[33] As Eckhart Tolle says: "Not to be able to stop thinking is a dreadful affliction, but we don't realize this because almost everyone is suffering from it, so it is considered normal." Tolle, Eckhart. *The Power of Now*. Novato, CA: New World Library, 1999

[34] Rick Hanson writes about the healing power of stillness in an article called "Find Stillness." *Psychology Today*. Mar 24, 2014. Web.

[35] Ibid

[36] Ibid

[37] Sarno, John. *Healing Back Pain, Healing Back Pain: The Mind-Body Connection*. New York City: Grand Central Publishing, Hachette Book Group, 1991. In this groundbreaking work, Dr. Sarno explores the mind-body connection between unconscious (and conscious) rage and many physical ailments.

[38] Wilhelm, Richard, trans. *The I-Ching or Book of Changes*. The Richard Wilhelm Translation rendered into English by Cary F. Baynes. Foreword by C.G. Jung. London: Routledge & Kegan Paul Ltd, 1971.

[39] In an article on the Buddhist Portal, Bill Scheffel writes about a different hexagram, called "Nourishment," in which he says: "In terms of meditation this might mean having a firm

seat and nurturing stillness while at the same time accommodating thoughts, including when our mind runs wild. It could also simply be a reminder to practice since movement is "within" (the lower hexagram) while stillness is "without" (the upper hexagram). So often when we are excessively discursive and emotional is the time when we should sit but we don't." Scheffel, Bill. "Meditation & Divination: A Review of the Taoist I Ching." Book review on Buddhist Portal. Web. August 31, 2016.

[40] For example, in a *Lifehack* article (June 21, 2018) titled "Science Says Silence Is Much More Important to Our Brains Than We Think," author Rebecca Beris describes a 2001 study that showed even when the brain was "resting" it was perpetually active internalizing and evaluating information. In 2013, in *Frontiers in Human Neuroscience*, it was reported that the brain's default mode network "is observed most closely during the psychological task of reflecting on one's personalities and characteristics (self-reflection), rather than during self-recognition, thinking of the self-concept, or thinking about self-esteem, for example." In other words, when the brain rests it is able to integrate internal and external information into "a conscious workspace."

[41] In the *Crooked Cucumber: The Life and Zen Teaching of Shunryu Suzuki*, the writer Chadwick describes Suzuki's zazen teaching: ""Suzuki had great respect for the difficulty of changing one's course, for the tenacity of habit, the addictiveness of thoughts and beliefs, the power of delusion. He was always teaching the importance of developing good habits so as not to become lost and confused, the importance of not wanting too much—this was called following the precepts. 'Make your best effort,' he said. But still he cautioned not to try too hard, saying that we would naturally follow the precepts if we just relaxed within our practice." p 301

[42] Gohman, Julie. Book review of "Silence: The Power of Quiet in a World Full of Noise" by Thich Nhat Hanh. *The Journal*

---

of Transpersonal Psychology, 2015, Vol. 47, No. 2. Web. May 30, 2018.

[43] Tara Brach, interviewed by Nora Krug in the *Washington Post,* Dec 2, 2016.

[44] Charles Ridley describes it this way: ""Breath is the mother and stillness the father, and together they create a polar process that organizes the wholeness of life. In this matrix, every subtle change in one part affects and modifies all other parts. The interconnecting fibers emerge out of a dynamic tension of opposites between unmanifest stillness and expressed form." Ridley, ch 1

[45] "The Breath of Life ... fulfills a basic human longing for union with its source. Like a well-tended seed, it creates your body, continues to grow as the roots of your health and perceptual integrity, and then it flowers on a universal scale, as your consciousness evolves beyond egocentricity to embrace the whole." Ridley, ch 2

[46] Wright, Patricia C. and Richard D. Wright. *The Divining Heart: Dowsing and Spiritual Unfoldment.* Rochester, VT: Destiny Books 1994, ch 8

[47] *The Cosmic Code: Quantum Physics as the Language of Nature,* by Heinz R. Pagels p 43 1992 Dover Publications. It's described as "one of the most important books on quantum mechanics ever written for lay readers ... Pagels, discusses and explains the core concepts of physics without resorting to complicated mathematics."

[48] Moore, Ruth. *Niels Bohr: The Man, His Science, & the World They Changed.* New York City: Alfred A. Knopf, 1966. Print. p.196. One of my favorite quotes from Bohr is: ""How wonderful that we have met with a paradox. Now we have some hope of making progress."

[49] Wikipedia tries to explain what is meant here by describing wave–particle duality as the concept in quantum mechanics that every particle or quantum entity can be described in terms not only of particles but also of waves. The challenge is that science demands we describe the behavior of quantum-scale objects either as a particle *or a*

wave. "It seems as though we must use sometimes the one theory and sometimes the other, while at times we may use either. We are faced with a new kind of difficulty. We have two contradictory pictures of reality; separately neither of them fully explains the phenomena of light, but together they do."
https://en.wikipedia.org/wiki/Wave%E2%80%93particle_duality

[50] Harrison, p 116

[51] Sion, ch 14

[52] Rothenberg, Albert. 1971. "The Process of Janusian Thinking in Creativity." *Archives of General Psychiatry*. 1971. Web. July 19, 2018. p 195).

[53] Shokek, p 80

[54] Aristotle, Metaphysics: Book XII, part 7

[55] Heidegger, p 68

[56] Long, p 35

[57] The word intuition comes from the Latin *intuir*, which means 'knowledge from within.' It is different from logical or informational knowledge. William James first explored the concept that cognition takes place in two different modes: "Intuition works in an associative manner: it feels effortless (even though it does use a significant amount of brain power), and it's fast. Rational thinking, on the contrary, is analytical, requires effort, and is slow." Both modes, however, work equally well in term of outcome. "Cognitive scientists think of intuition as a set of nonconscious cognitive and affective processes; the outcome of these processes is often difficult to articulate and is not based on deliberate thinking, but it's real and ... effective nonetheless." Popova, Maria. "The Science and Philosophy of Friendship: Lessons from Aristotle on the Art of Connection." *Brainpickings*. Sep 19, 2013. Web.

[58] In an interesting paper published by the *Journal for the Association of Transpersonal Psychologists*, the authors discuss the psychologist Aratesh's criticism of the Western tendency for placing excessive emphasis on instruction and

neglecting the wisdom of intuition and insight: "The intuitive individual is aware of the duality of thinking: 'that which is made by the mind and that which is made by the heart.' The heart, according to Arasteh, is the power that utilizes all other faculties as its servants or instruments." Knabb, Joshua J., and Robert K. Welsh. "Reconsidering A. Reza Arasteh: Sufism and Psychotherapy." *The Journal of Transpersonal Psychology*. Vol. 41 — 1. 2009.

[59] Byron Katie, p 7

[60] *Tao* means the Path or the Way. It refers to a power that envelops, surrounds, and flows through all things, living and nonliving. It regulates natural processes and nourishes balance in the universe. It embodies a harmony of opposites (there's no love without hate, no light without dark, no yang without yin), which transcends the dualistic thinking that creates so much suffering in our psyches.

[61] *The I-Ching*: Even while we need to 'go with the flow', the I-Ching teaches us that we also need to plan in advance and consider carefully each action before making it. In the I-Ching, the patterns of change are symbolized by solid (yang) and broken (yin) lines that are combined to show 64 relationships of correlative forces and are known as the hexagrams. Dao is the alteration of these forces, most often often stated as yin and yang. Correlatives in Daoism are not opposites, mutually excluding each other, as the experience of stillness in movement expresses. They represent the ebb and flow of the forces of reality: yin/yang, male/female; excess/decrease; leading/following; active/passive. As we approach the fullness of yang, yin begins to emerge. Thus stillness is in motion and motion is in stillness throughout our lives. Chuang Tsu tells the story of the Master asking his student, Yen Hui, to describe his experience of stillness. "I forget my body and senses, and leave all appearance and information behind. In the middle of Nothing, I join the Source of All Things," replies Yen Hui. The Master bows to him and tells him: "You have transcended the limitations of time and knowledge. I am

far behind you. You have found the Way!" *Tao Te Ching*, ch 48

62 *Miriam-Rose Ungunmerr-Baumann, a Ngangiwumirr Elder,* as quoted in an article by Jonathan Davis titled "Australian Aboriginals Know the Healing Power of Listening in Stillness". Found in "An Indigenous Approach to Healing Trauma." *Uplift.* Jul 20, 2015.

63 *Jonathan Davis.* "An Indigenous Approach to Healing Trauma." *Uplift.* Jul 20, 2015.

64 *Ibid.* The actual quote from Stanley Grof is: "The initial moment of pain may have become so overwhelming that we make a subconscious decision to 'check out'; in other words, we emotionally dissociate. Every part of us screams 'Stop, I don't want to feel this!' The problem is that we don't *stop* the emotional experience, we just press *pause.*"

65 *Ibid.*

66 Long, Max Freedom. *The Secret Science Behind Miracles.* New York: Simon & Schuster. Ch 1

67 I describe my experience with Huna and some of the teachings I learned about Hawaiian spirituality in an earlier book I wrote called *What Would You Do If There Was Nothing You Had To Do? Practices to create your life the way you want it to be.* Alford, MA: WriteSpa Press, 2012. Print. p 15.

68 Blackburn, Stewart. "Nalu as a way of stillness." Message to the Author. July 24, 2018. Email. 7/24/18. A Kahuna master, Stewart calls himself the Shaman of Pleasure; he is a writer, teaching, and spiritual counselor. His passion is to bring everyone to their essential experience of happiness, which he believes is our birthright.

69 Kaila Hawai'i: January 29, 2010 Hawaiian word-of-the-day. https://kailahawaii.wordpress.com.

70 Marko Pogacnik. *Nature Spirits & Elemental Beings: Working with the Intelligence in Nature.* Findhorn, Scotland: Findhorn Press, 1997. p 17

71 From an email sent to me from Tobias Kaye, dated May 2, 2019: "There are three aspects of the Self that we all experience to

*a greater or lesser degree. The soul-body entity is a landscape
with a lake – the etheric body. The lake is held by land – the
physical body. Over the lake the air passes, lit by moon and stars.
Stillness allows the winds of the astral body to abate. In a short
time, the surface of the lake becomes calm and mirrors the moon.
The image of the moon in the lake appears to us as beguilingly
beautiful. The everyday self, our normal identity can be seen in
this way. When we are upset, we lose sight of who we are and act
out of the distress rather than out of a clear image of who we
know ourselves to be. The moon is not dependent on the weather
and even when obscured by clouds is always there. I compare this
to the higher self, the identity that creates our daytime self and
remains true from life to life, creating in each new lake a new
image of itself. The light of the moon is not its own light. Moon
reflects sun. Our eternal or higher self is in its turn dependent on
the Christ or Universal Human I. Thus my essential humanity
lives equally in you. My eternal being is steady and reliable, the
source of my everyday self. My everyday self depends on my
stillness to be present in my actions."*

[72] https://en.wikipedia.org/wiki/Stopping_by_Woods_on_a_
Snowy_Evening

[73] Rae Chandran during a workshop in Pittsfield, MA, in
November, 2015. raechandran.com

[74] Masaru Emoto. *The Hidden Messages in Water.* Atria Books;
September 20, 2005.

[75] Transpersonal psychologist Wallach describes spirituality as
'having as a common definitional core, some experiential,
notional, behavioral, or intentional relationship with some
transcendent reality, out of which arises meaning, solace,
or motivation for an individual.' Friedman, Harris L., and
Hartelius, Glen, editors. *The Wiley Blackwell Handbook of
Transpersonal Psychology.* Chichester, UK: John Wiley &
Sons, 2015. Print. p 581.

[76] Hoff, Benjamin. *The Tao of Pooh.* p 150.

[77] Keats, John. *The Complete Poetical Works and Letters of John
Keats.* Cambridge Edition. Boston, MA: Houghton, Mifflin
and Company, 2012. p 277.

78 Klein, Jean. *Listening*. Nonduality Press. ch 1.

79 *The Thundering Years: Rituals and Sacred Wisdom for Teens.* by Julie Tallard Johnson. 2001

80 Steiner, Rudolf. *Observations on Adolescence*. AWSNA Press 2001 Fair Oaks, CA

81 Williams-Siegfredsen, J. (2013). *Understanding the Danish forest school approach: Early years education in practice.* 10.4324/9780203136034. "Written to support the work of all those in the field of early years education and childcare, this is a vital text for students, early years and childcare practitioners, teachers, early years professionals, children's centre professionals, lecturers, advisory teachers, head teachers and setting managers." Retrieved from researchgate.net.

82 Studies have shown how children learn better, are more socially confident and calm, symptoms of ADHD are reduced, their focus improves so they do better on tests, bullying and child obesity is reduced, and other psychological and physical health benefits continue to be explored and proven. Walker, Timothy D. "Kindergarten, Naturally." Article in *The Atlantic*. Sept. 15, 2016.

83 Eckhart Tolle, *Stillness Speaks*, ch 7

84 Marcus E. Raichle, "The Brain's Dark Energy," *Scientific American*, March 2010.

85 Fadiman, James and Robert Frager (editors). Foreword by Huston Smith. *Essential Sufism*. HarperOne: November 17, 1999. The actual quote the Master said is: "If you have never trodden the path of love, go away and fall in love; then come back and see us."

86 Solovyov, Vladimir. *The Meaning of Love*. Introduction by Owen Barfield. Lindisfarne Books.

87 Ibid

88 Tolle, *Stillness Speaks*, ch 8

89 Wilson, Brian and Asher, Tony. "Don't Talk (Put Your Head On My Shoulder)." Lyrics © Universal Music Publishing Group. July 18, 1966.

90 Qtd. in William James, *Varieties of Religious Experience*. p 261.

[91] Dr Leon Masters describes the mystical state as love: "When mystics through the ages have tried to express what they experienced as being God's Presence, they could only describe it as oneness with all and, in that absolute oneness—absolute love." *Mystical Insights.* ch. 47

[92] Bailey, Alice A. *Esoteric Healing. Volume IV: A Treatise on the Seven Rays.* New York City: Lucis Publishing Company, 1998.

[93] There are many, many ways to experience romantic love, with all the ecstasy, suffering, and yearning that it offers us in life. My own personal transformational experiences of romantic love have mostly occurred in dreams, visions, and meditation. Here is one of them: One morning I experienced an extraordinary vision of an enormous white-feathered bird with a dark head. It was as least twice as big as I was. The love emanating from this creature drew me toward it, and I placed my cheek on the softness of its white-feathered breast. The feathers were so real, so soft and white, and the love that emanated from this creature for me was beyond anything I can describe. The feeling I had for this great being was equally powerful—passion, romance, and requited love vibrated in every cell. The feeling was like the swelling of a symphonic orchestra getting louder and louder, filling me, but instead of with sound, it was with Love. Being so in love, and being beloved, overtook everything else in my life, no matter how overwhelming, exhausting, or dull. Instead, for a long time afterward, I felt color, gentleness, and warmth around me. All sounds were sweeter, all colors brighter, the sky and trees bent over me with grace and protectiveness, the earth was my home and I was happy in it. I describe this experiences as a reminder to keep yourself open to realms of possibility in romance that you may not have thought of before. Some people may have a romance with a garden, a tree, a cause. Don't limit yourself to one person or a Grimm's fairy-tale ideal.

94 I found it interesting that Bruno's research connects people who tend to get Lyme as being healers. Here's her full article: https://laurabruno.wordpress.com/2009/09/24/healing-lyme-disease/

95 Eliot, Jane Winslow. *How to Begin—Whatever Your Age.* Northampton, MA: 1984. Unpublished.

96 Transpersonal psychologists Joshua Knabb and Robert Welsh describe how helpful it is for dying individuals to regard themselves as part of a much bigger whole: "The individual is able to see life as continuous and extending beyond death in a transcendent fashion, that is, the cosmic or universal self. The mortality of humankind is seen as a stepping-stone toward something greater than the materialistic world. In other words, the aspirant 'can visualize himself and measure his death in terms of humanity foreseeing that death is not powerful when man becomes mankind'." Knabb, Joshua J., and Robert K. Welsh. "Reconsidering A. Reza Arasteh: Sufism and Psychotherapy." *The Journal of Transpersonal Psychology.* Vol. 41—1. 2009. n.p.

97 "Transcendence of death, pain, sickness, evil, etc., when one is at a level high enough to be reconciled with the necessity of death, pain, etc. From a Godlike, or Olympian point of view, these are necessary, and can be understood as necessary. If this attitude is achieved, as for instance it can be in the recognition, then bitterness, rebelliousness, anger, resentment may all disappear or at least be much lessened." Maslow, Abraham H. *The Farther Reaches of Human Nature.* New York City: Penguin Books, 1971. p 261.

98 Patricia and David Wright describe the experience of stillness in dowsing: "For one timeless moment you are offered a glimpse not of the point of stillness but of the Source of that point of stillness. After you have experienced the stillness at the center of your own being, you will then learn to perceive the stillness at the heart of everything outside your own self. Then you will begin to sense and resonate with the fabric of

interconnectedness joining all those essential forces of matter." Wright, Patricia C., and Richard D. Wright. *The Divining Heart: Dowsing and Spiritual Unfoldment.* Rochester, Vermont: Destiny books. Introduction

[99] In Stanislav Grof's words: "Spiritual opening often takes the form of a spiral combining regression and progression, rather than a strictly linear fashion. Particularly frequent is then opening involving psychospiritual death and rebirth, in which case the critical interface between the personal and transpersonal is the perinatal level. This can be supported not just by clinical observations, but also by the study of the lives of mystics, such as St Teresa of Avila, St John of the Cross, and others." Grof, Stanislav. *A Brief History of Transpersonal Psychology.* Retrieved from stanislavgrof.com. n.d. Web. May 29, 2018. p 13

[100] Tolle, *Stillness Speaks*, ch 4

[101] Ibid, ch 7

[102] In this way, we transcend the concept of duality *and* the concept of fate versus free will. Instead we fuse with our inherent nature and live our destiny I love how Abraham Maslow describes this: "To transcend one's will ... to yield to one's destiny or fate and to fuse with it, to love it in the Spinoza sense or in the Taoistic sense. To embrace, lovingly, one's own destiny." Maslow, Abraham. *The Farther Reaches of Human Nature.* New York City: Penguin Books, 1971. p 264.

[103] Aristotle. *Nicomachean Ethics.* (W. D. Ross, Trans.). n.d. Retrieved from The Internet Classics Archive. http://classics.mit.edu. Book X, part 8

[104] Carl Rogers, qtd Schillings, Astrid. "Stillness and Awareness from Person to Person." *Focusing.org.* 2012. Web. July 14, 2018

[105] Harrison, p 115

[106] Psalm 46:10

[107] Rudolf Steiner said in one of his lectures: "The totality of truth is present in every soul as a seed and can be brought to blossom if the soul devotes itself to the development of

that seed." From a lecture he gave called *"Background to the Gospel of St Mark."* Thirteen lectures given in Berlin, Munich, Hanover, and Coblenz, between 17 October, 1910 and 10 June, 1911; translated by E.H. Goddard and D.S. Osmond. London: Rudolf Steiner Press, 1968. Retrieved from rsarchive.org. Web. p. 184

[108] Harrison, p 109-110

[109] According to Harrison, "quantum physics describes some elements of a new medical paradigm. The subatomic universe is a world where nothing has inherent location or physicality without the application of observation. This observation alters the probable world into a definite world." Ibid, p 112

[110] "The subatomic universe is described as existing without location, inseparable, and without objective nature. The farthest edge of science begins to look like the world described by mystics." Ibid, p 113

[111] "Physicists had discovered that their very presence—that is the presence of consciousness—profoundly affected the quantifiable reality they were observing." Ibid, p 111

[112] Transpersonal psychologist John Davis writes: "I count nonduality as spirituality's most central insight. Ultimately and fundamentally, each part is part of the whole, and the whole is nondualistic." Davis, John, Ph.D. "We Keep Asking Ourselves, What Is Transpersonal Psychology?" *Nonduality*. Web. Reprinted from *Noumenon: Newsletter for the Nondual Perspective*. June 17, 2018. https://www.nonduality.com/tp.htm

[113] Carl Jung, qtd. in Clark, Margaret's article called "Our Spiritual Needs." *Society of Analytical Psychology – Jungian Psychology and Analysis.* n.d. Jung also says: "Individuation means becoming an 'individual,' and, in so far as 'individuality' embraces our innermost, last, and incomparable uniqueness, it also implies becoming one's own self. We could therefore translate individuation as 'coming to selfhood' or 'self-realization'."

[114] Ibid.

[115] Yogananda, Paramahansa. *Stillness*. Yogananda.com.au. n.p./n/d. Web. July 13, 2018.

[116] Masters, Dr. Leon. "Masters Degree Curriculum." University of Sedona. Sedona, AZ. 2:70.

[117] Aristotle. *Metaphysics*. Book IX, part 8

[118] Aristotle. *Physics*. Book VIII, part 9. He goes on in part 10: "We have three things, the movement, the moved, and thirdly that in which the motion takes place, namely the time: and these are either all infinite or all finite or partly — that is to say two of them or one of them — finite and partly infinite."

[119] Shokek, Shimon. *Kabbalah and the Art of Being: The Smithsonian Lectures*. New York City: Routledge, 2001. p 79—80. He goes on to describe the principle of change and stillness: "As Aristotle claims, those things that exist by nature and do not have an external cause, have within themselves *the principle of change and stillness*. Hence, the nature of God and man can be described in Aristotelian terms as a source or cause of being moved and of being still … in virtue of itself, and not in virtue of an associated exterior attribute. … God dwells in the realm of change and stillness at once: He resides simultaneously in the domain of pregnancy and the domain of giving birth. His awakening is not characterized in Kabbalah as a single event that occurred."

[120] Grof, p 1. Maslow's actual words are: "The old psychology did not help people to understand their qualities of 'love, self-consciousness, self-determination, personal freedom, morality, art, philosophy, religion, and science' as part of their psychological make-up and well-being."

[121] Grof, p 3.

[122] Davis, John, Ph.D. "We Keep Asking Ourselves, What Is Transpersonal Psychology?" *Nonduality*. Web. Reprinted from *Noumenon: Newsletter for the Nondual Perspective*. June 17, 2018.

[123] Grof, p 5.

[124] Friedman & Hartelius, p 9.

---

[125] Friedman & Hartelius, p 18. In an article in *The Humanistic Psychologist*, the authors define transpersonal psychology as "beyond-ego psychology, integrative/holistic psychology, and psychology of transformation." Essentially, we "share a vision of the world as a vibrant, alive, and intelligent community … whether it is the insight of the unconscious mind, the wisdom of the body, the cultural repositories built up within human culture, or the adaptive capacities of the ecosystem."

[126] Ibid, p 11

[127] Ibid. "As an integrative/holistic pursuit, transpersonal psychology examines the phenomena of psyche as elements that belong not merely to the ego, but to larger contexts as well: the living body in its entirety, the therapeutic relationship, the social and ecological situation, or the greater-than-human matrix of existence." p 12

www.ingramcontent.com/pod-product-compliance
Lightning Source LLC
Chambersburg PA
CBHW030913090426
42737CB00007B/183